Deterrent

R. Merial Martin

PublishAmerica
Baltimore

First printing

ISBN: 1-4137-6582-3
PUBLISHED BY PUBLISHAMERICA, LLLP
www.publishamerica.com
Baltimore

Printed in the United States of America

The Link

The Maryland governor, Sanford Booth, maintains a satellite office in downtown Baltimore. Gloria Young, Booth's secretary, is working late and singing to herself while she types. It is the evening of March 16, 2011. Secret Service Agent Herman walks into her office. It had been easy for him to gain admission past the guard on the bottom floor of the governor's office complex. As a secret service agent, he would never be questioned. Herman had visited the office several times before.

"Evening, Miss Young."

"Hello, Agent Herman. The governor is not in. Oh! But I guess you know that already. 'Cause he just left to go home before he goes to Camp David."

She hurriedly rearranges her desk, giving the appearance that she had been tremendously busy while covering up the fact that she had been singing into the recorder-phone.

"Yeah, I know, but I came to tell the governor that he's not invited this weekend."

"Well, unless you catch him at home, he'll be there anyway. But tell me—why not? He's the president's best friend and goes there all the time."

With a hardened facial expression, he tells her, "Don't worry about the reason, Miss Young, you just be certain to remember that he is not invited. Just remember that, like he was never invited. Got that?"

5

Gloria is on her way outside the governor's office building, and upon opening the door to her car, a vehicle speeds towards her with lights flashing in her eyes. She runs to the front of the car and falls to the ground, just in time to avoid the impact of the vehicle ramming into the driver's side of her car. Nearly in shock, she scurries to the door and is pulling the handle but cannot open the damaged door. The vehicle wheels around and charges towards her as she manages to open the door, get in, and slide to the passenger side. She ducks her head as silencer shots are fired into her car. Scared, she leaves through the passenger door and runs back into the building. The vehicle speeds off, then stops.

Back in her office, she frantically dials the phone number of the building security and then stops as she notices that her appointment book has pages torn out that are all over her desk. As she pieces them together, she sees that March 15th and 16th are missing. She goes to the window and sees Agent Herman patting the back of the driver of the vehicle who tried to kill her. The building security guard is standing nearby, too.

"Why? Why?" she sobs. She watches as the car drives away. *It was like they wanted me to see them,* she thinks.

Gloria goes back to her desk and piles personal belongings into her large shoulder bag.

"Oh!" she sighs, and drops her bag when she hears a clicking sound like the cocking of a pistol. But it turns out to be the answer phone, which was set for conference-call taping. She remembers that she had been taping her singing right before Herman walked in and forgot to turn it off. Grabbing the cassette, which she also knows would contain the messages of the 15th and 16th, she runs out of the office. The streets are clear of traffic, but she decides to forego getting to her car and takes the rear exit to hail a cab.

In the apartment, which she shares with a roommate, Gina, she is hurriedly packing two suitcases. Hearing the front door lock turn, she drops to the floor beside her bed.

"Gloria, are you home?" calls Gina.

She recognizes Gina's voice. Gina is in the kitchenette talking aloud about the bargains that she found at the supermarket. Understanding that Gina obviously is alone, Gloria walks to the doorway where she can see Gina unpacking groceries. Trembling as she approaches, she asks, "Gina, are you alone?"

"Sure, girl, this is shopping night, not party night. Hey, what's the matter? Why do you look so pale? Gee, Gloria, you're trembling something fierce."

"I have to leave town, the Secret Service tried to kill me tonight and I don't know why."

"Call the police," advises Gina, as she reaches for the wall telephone.

"No!" cries Gloria as she grabs Gina's arm. "I've got to get out of town."

Moving to her side and placing a sympathetic arm around her shoulder, she says, "Where will you go?"

"I don't know, maybe to the West Coast."

"Say, girl, I can see that you're serious. I wish I could help."

Gina moves to the counter and pulls out her wallet from her purse.

"Say, here's Al's card, you know, my ex in L.A. If you make it there, look him up and he'll help you to lay low."

As her bus arrives in Memphis, Tennessee, the next night, Gloria gets off for a layover. While walking back to board again, she picks up a newspaper and reads the headlines about her boss being arrested. On the same page is an article about the killing of her roommate, Gina.

"They were after me," she cries aloud. Frantically, she runs to board the bus headed for Los Angeles.

The Trial

The halls of the Federal Court in Washington, DC, are overcrowded. Reporters nearly outnumber the spectators. Television cameramen are adjusting their equipment by panning the crowd and zeroing on their newscasters. Attorney James Webb, a former Harvard Law professor, approaches the court room doors. The cameramen focus on him. Reporters push and shove to get their microphones near him. Webb is a personal friend and counselor to Governor Sanford Booth, who is on trial for an assassination attempt on the President of the United States.

Reporters shout questions to Webb.

"I hear you have new evidence to clear the governor?"

"Mr. Webb? Mr. Webb? The special prosecutor stated that the governor is guilty and there is no way the jury will free him. Can you comment?"

Webb raises his arm to quiet the throng of shouting reporters.

"I have only one comment to make. Quiet! Please! It is just as I orated in my opening statement to the jury over a month ago: Governor Booth has been framed by high government officials and it will be my duty to convince the jury that the governor is innocent. That is all, ladies and gentlemen. That is all I have to say."

Reporters begin shouting questions again, as Webb struggles through the crowd to get through the double doors that lead to the courtroom.

"Who are those officials, Mr. Webb?"

"Are they the same people who made the other two attempts on the life of the president?"

"Can you give us their names, Mr. Webb?"

As Webb walks through the doors, he turns and replies, "No comment."

Reporters are shouting questions while they make their way into the courtroom to take their places. This noise and state of disorganization causes the bailiffs to rush to the doors to quiet them and to direct them in an orderly fashion to an area set aside for the press. The judge officiating this trial has allowed for live coverage by the news media. The courtroom fills up rapidly. Three senators and two congressmen along with others members of the president's staff come into the courtroom and take their seats in the front row. Reporters take pictures of the entourage. Two seats remain vacant on that row. The double doors open wide as secret servicemen fill up the doorway and scan the audience. Out of the middle of that group comes the President of the United States, Richard Morton, and the Vice President, James Mokski. Again the cameras flash as reporters take pictures and focus their television cameras in the direction of the president.

"All rise for the President of the United States," shouts the head bailiff.

President Morton and the vice president take their seats in the front row behind the prosecutor's table.

The courtroom is buzzing with conversations throughout the audience. Mokski and the president engage in mouth-to-ear whispers. Senator Bynam from the state of Maryland where Booth is governor is speaking to Senator Grogan from Massachusetts.

"It looks bad for Sandy," says Grogan in a Boston brogue, "the president's testimony should seal his fate."

"It does look bad," whispers Bynam.

"Sandy told me that he has been framed and most of the evidence that the prosecutor has brought forth is circumstantial. Even so, Sandy is relying on the president's testimony to clear him."

President Morton and Mokski are still whispering, back and forth.

"Mr. President, you have a duty to perform for the American people and for your safety and the health of your wife. The prosecutor has tried to tie Booth to all three attempts on your life. He has only the evidence on this last one, but that doesn't mean Booth couldn't have been involved or directed the other two. All you have to do is tell the truth about what happened at Camp David."

"Jim, it's still hard to believe that my strongest supporter and best friend through the years is responsible for these attempts. I just hope his attorney has the evidence to prove the prosecutor wrong. How do you feel about this case, Jim?" whispers the president.

"Mr. President, I think—"

The vice president is interrupted by the flashing of cameras as a bailiff, holding the arm of Governor Booth, leads him to a chair next to Counselor Webb. The governor looks towards the president as he is walking across the courtroom. Once seated, he turns and gains eye contact with Morton, who nods his head, affirmatively, and Booth smiles and gives a sigh of relief.

Still waiting for the appearance of the judge, Booth, a Harrison Ford lookalike and thirty-seven years old, sits pensively looking at the jury, which is comprised of three elderly black women, four black men, one Oriental man, two young white women, and two elderly white men. The person in the foreman's seat is a young black man in his thirties.

"All rise, First Federal District Court, in and for the District of Columbia, Judge George Wallingsford presiding, is now in session," shouts the head bailiff.

Judge Wallingsford is wheeled into the courtroom up a special ramp leading to the bench by a bailiff.

"Take your seats, please," announces the judge, just as the audience is rising. Wheeling himself into a position facing the audience, he straightens papers on the desk. He is grey-haired, sixty-two years of age, and paralyzed from an auto accident. He looks over the rim of his Ben Franklin half-moon glasses in the direction of Morton and says, "Good morning, Mr. President, you honor us with your presence in this court. I know that you had requested not to be a part of this trial in person, however, the Defense subpoenaed you in an unusual request, and so in the interest of justice, we welcome you."

President Morton nods in acknowledgment. The judge turns to the jury and sternly tells them, "I must counsel you, ladies and gentlemen of the jury, not to be intimidated or impressed by the status of the next witness, but to continue to weigh the evidence that has been presented here in the last 30 days and any testimony given today as you have previously, without regard for the position of the witness. Since the prosecution rested their case on yesterday, it is time for the defense to present their case. With that said, Mr. Van de Kamp," inquiring of the prosecutor, "are you ready?"

"Ready to proceed, your honor," replies the prosecutor.

"Whenever you're ready, Mr. Webb. Call your next witness."

Standing at the defense table, Webb begins, "Your honor, the defense," a resounding emphasis is placed on the word *defense*, "calls the honorable Richard Morton, President of the United States."

"Objection!" shouts Van de Kamp.

"Mr. Van de Kamp, are you objecting to the witness being allowed to testify?" shouts the judge.

"Not so, your honor" replies the prosecutor. "I only make reference to your instructions to the jury not to be impressed by the title of the witness and I feel the defense is trying to void your counsel to them."

Webb has a long smirk on his face.

"Mr. Webb, the bench could get that same impression from the enunciations made by you, however, I believe the jury to be wise and that they are considering statements and presence as I have advised. Objection denied. The witness will come forth."

President Morton stands and the cameras begin to flash.

"I caution the press to cease from using the flash cameras. The lights from the TV cameras are sufficient. I realize the importance of the coverage of this trial for the benefit of the citizens of this country, but I will not tolerate interruptions or distractions.

"A word to the wise," the judge demands.

The president is seated on the witness stand as the head bailiff walks in front of him and asks, "Sir, please you raise your right hand? Do you swear that the testimony you are about to give is the truth, the whole truth, and nothing but the truth, so help you God?"

"I do," replies the president.

Webb walks in front of the witness box to begin his questioning of the president.

"Mr. President, how long have you known the defendant, Governor Sanford Booth?"

"I've know Sandy for over twenty-five years."

"Thank you, sir. We have read and seen your account of what happened over seven months ago, or more specifically, March 17, 2011, but in your own words, for the benefit of national TV and more importantly for the benefit of the judge and jury, please state the events leading up to and including that day as you recall them?"

"Objection!" interrupts the prosecutor. "Your honor, counsel is forcing the witness to make a statement, and shouldn't the witness be informed that he can answer only yes or no questions?"

"Mr. Prosecutor, what law school did you go to? No, don't answer that," quips the judge, "Objection overruled, take your time, sir, and tell us, just as you recall, what happened on March 17, 2011."

"Well, it was St. Patrick's Day, and I had decided to spend the day at Camp David. It had been a short winter and the onset of spring had brought good weather to the camp. I had invited some of our Irish Republicans to spend the day with my family. The camp is well secured so I had a habit of taking long walks alone over the grounds in the mornings. Some of the guests had arrived, but I had not seen them all yet; we were to get together for a brunch and some parade watching on TV at 9 a.m. I could hear shotgun blasts coming from the rear of the property where we have a skeet shooting range. The shooting is supervised by one or more secret service agents. They never allowed me to shoot, unless I was there alone, that is without any guests. Oh, except for the vice president, Governor Booth, Secretary of State Bill Marshall or my wife. If any of those people were with me, they tolerated it. It was about 6 a.m., and I had decided to start back to the main house. Moving through the trees, I recall the shooting had stopped. Then, I heard a shot and the trees and bushes around me seemed to tear up. Leaves were flying in the air. I realized that shot was at me and almost instinctively, I dove to the ground as another blast went over my head. Some of the buckshot grazed me. I guess my rear end was too big. I crawled behind a tree, looked up, and saw a man in an orange jacket running towards the tree area where I was. I screamed for help and fell to the ground again. I stayed down for about a minute until I heard the voices of secret service agents. I stood up to see a man in the orange jacket running back towards the skeet range. Three agents took off after him. The next thing I knew, the agents were bringing Sandy to the main house. He was handcuffed. One of them had a shotgun and Sandy was wearing that orange jacket that he always wore. But I had not invited Sandy. He wasn't supposed to be here, I thought. I asked Agent Herman, the chief agent on the premises, what they were doing with the governor. He told me that they were arresting him for an assassination attempt on my life. Sandy spoke up and tried to say that he didn't have anything to do with the shooting, in fact that he was chasing someone when the agents caught up to him. Agent Herman hit Sandy in the mouth and told him to shut up and that he would have a chance to speak, but only to a lawyer. Herman had other agents take Sandy to the security area at Camp David. I was disturbed by the whole scene. I did ask Herman to double check the grounds. The next thing I knew, I was in a helicopter and headed back to the White House. That's what I remember about March 17."

"Thank you, Mr. President," Webb cuts him off.

"Sir, I don't know what your feelings for Governor Booth have been since that date, but can you tell us what your relationship was like prior to March 17th?"

"Sure, Sandy was one of my top supporters and I was of his career, also. As I said, we go back, politically, to when I was a junior congressman and he was a student campaign worker while in college. Later I supported him for city alderman, state secretary, and then governor. He helped me carry many states in the east and southeast when I ran for president. Sandy and his wife, June, were our very best friends. I say were, because June died some three years ago and that hurt us all."

"Thank you, sir," Webb breaks in.

"Did you recognize your longtime friend as the man in the orange jacket who was shooting at you or when you got to your feet to see him running away?"

The president pauses and says, "No, I did not."

"That's all I have, your honor," states Webb.

The president appears in awe, and says, "But are you through?"

Judge Wallingsford breaks in, "Mr. President, Mr. Webb has concluded. Now, Mr. Van de Kamp, you may cross examine."

"Your honor," replies the prosecutor, "I would like to pass at this time, but would like to reserve the right to recall before summation."

"That's irregular, Mr. Van de Kamp, but I will allow a recall, if requested. Mr. President, you may step down, sir. I know you have a busy schedule, but for the sake of justice, I will try to move both counsel to speedier decisions. Would both counsel approach the bench."

President Morton returns to his seat, and Mokski bends over the banister and asks, "I wonder why the prosecutor didn't question you. He may be making a big mistake." Mokski looks towards Booth. Their eyes make contact, and when Booth smiles, Mokski returns an affirmative nod, but being wary that others might notice. Upon looking away from Booth, his face shows signs of dismay and confusion as to whether the prosecutor has given up. *Booth feels I'm on his side*, he thinks, *but if he only knew.*

At the bench, the judge asks, "Van de Kamp, I don't understand your procedures, don't you realize the president has a heart condition and we need to get him out of here and away from these cameras? Mr. Webb, who's next?"

"Sir, I only have the governor."

"No other witnesses on the governor's behalf?"

"No, sir, this is it."

"Very well, go back to your tables."

As they walk back, the Judge speaks, "Mr. Webb, the ball is in your court."

"Your honor, I'd like to call the Honorable Sanford Booth, governor of the great state of Maryland."

"Governor Booth, please?" sounds the Judge, while pointing to the witness chair.

Seated in the chair and under oath, Webb approaches him and asks, "Governor, did you on March 17, 2011, at Camp David, attempt to assassinate the President of the United States?"

"No, I did not."

"Governor, the president stated that you were not invited to Camp David, how did you happen to be there?"

"My secretary relayed to me a phone message from the White House that I was invited to spend the St. Patrick's Day at Camp David with the president …"

Governor Booth has a flashback to his office as his secretary, Gloria, is allowing the message to record and is taking the message conference type while she powders her nose.

"I have told you too many times, Gloria, to turn off that answer phone and speak directly with the callers. Now who was that message from?"

"From the White House, Governor. The president requests your presence at Camp David on St. Patrick's Day."

"OK, thank you, now write that down in your appointment book and cancel any appointments on the 17th, and stop being so forgetful."

"… I thought not to RSVP because many times I have been asked and just showed up there. There is always a guest list, but the agent at the gate did not have my name on it. He called the security post and then told me that Agent Herman said I was a good friend of the president and it was OK for me to enter. I didn't question that situation because it had happened before. After all, I was a friend who could be trusted."

"Did you seek out the president to question why your name was not on the list?"

"No! Mr. Webb, as I stated, it had happened before. I thought it was an oversight. His wife and children were never on the list, and I felt that

I was family, too."

"What time did you arrive?"

"It was about 5 a.m. I drove from the Capitol to Camp David."

"Then what did you do?"

"Just what I have always done on arrival, I went to the security post and checked out a shotgun, shells, and put on a jacket given me by Agent Herman. One of the agents walked to the course with me. It was about 5:45 a.m.; I remember that because I looked at my watch to see how long I had been out there. The agent pulled as I shot. I had stopped to help the agent reload the clays. It was about six a.m. when we heard a shot from up the hill towards the main house. I was walking towards the agent when a man in camouflage dress appeared and shot the agent. I saw him turn and run, so I ran to the agent's side. I could see he was dead. The shotgun blast had torn open his face. I took off after the man in the camouflage suit and I heard another shot from up the hill. The killer was running towards the house through the trees. I reached the top of the hill and could see the main house. Agents were running towards me about 100 yards away. I saw the killer running back down the hill. I started after him. Then I heard Agent Herman yell for me to drop my shotgun. I did, and before I knew it they were on top of me and put handcuffs on my wrists. Then they took me back to the main house where the president was waiting."

"Governor, did you tell them about the man you were chasing?"

"I tried, but as the president told you, they hit me and told me not to speak. The president asked Herman to let me talk and just as I was about to speak, one of the agents came up and reported that I had killed an agent on the skeet course. Things changed and I was not allowed to speak. I realized that I couldn't talk to the agents, because I knew one or more of them had to be involved. Otherwise, how could the killer I was chasing, or the man wearing an orange jacket who shot at the president have gotten into the compound? Now none of those agents can be found. I am told that they were transferred to foreign countries to protect ambassadors. And Agent Herman is supposed to have been killed by terrorists in Iraq."

"Governor, I ask you once again, under oath, did you on March 17,

2011, at Camp David, attempt to assassinate the President of the United States?"

Looking directly at President Morton, he admits, "I love this man like family; I was not involved in this attempt, or any others. I was only shooting skeet, and no, I did not and could not make such an attempt."

The president maintains a stoic look, but inside he is hurting with pain and desire to scream that he is positive that Sandy is innocent.

"Your witness," Webb says to Van de Kamp, staring at him confidently as he takes his seat while the prosecutor approaches the witness stand.

Van de Kamp has planned to antagonistically question the governor. After all, he has aspirations to ascend to the governorship of Maryland. He knew that if Booth were cleared that he had a hold on the job for the next four years. Even after that, he would be instrumental in getting his own candidate elected. But he couldn't wait that long. This was his opportunity to gain recognition as the people's attorney in this case and clear way for his bid for the governorship.

"Mr. Booth," he says, disdaining from referring to him as governor, "do you still contend that you received an invitation from the White House staff?"

"Yes, I do."

"How then do you account for the testimony previously given by Ms. Southfield, whom the president directed to call all Irish guests, when she testified under oath and produced this list, exhibit 15, which shows the names of the guests invited and called?"

"No comment on the list, but I do know that my secretary received a call and conveyed the message to me."

"And where is your secretary today, Mr. Booth?"

"I don't know."

"Is it true that your secretary has mysteriously disappeared after her roommate was murdered?"

"Yes, I heard that, but I have been in custody for the last six months without bail—how could I know where she is!"

"But, Mr. Booth, she is the only person who can corroborate your story as to what caused you to go to Camp David. Haven't you been concerned about her whereabouts?"

"Yes, I have, but the Feds and my attorney's staff has failed to find her."

"Mr. Booth, isn't it true that you fabricated this story and used your friendship with the president to gain entry into Camp David for the purpose of assassinating the man you despised because you lost the nomination of your party that he gained?"

"No."

"Isn't it true that you shot the agent on the skeet range and because you knew that the president took early morning walks alone that gave you the best chance to shoot him?"

"No, that's not true either."

"Objection!" screams Webb, but seemingly is not heard by the judge.

"Isn't true that you planned to shoot the president of the United States and blame it on the agent you killed on the skeet range?"

"No, that's not true either."

"Objection! Your honor," screams Webb, "the prosecutor is badgering the defendant."

"Mr. Van de Kamp," says the judge in a reprimanding tone, "you may continue, but I caution you."

"Mr. Booth, in your testimony, you stated that you drove from your office to Camp David. You mean to tell the jurors and the high government officials that as governor, you were not chauffeured, but that you actually drove the vehicle yourself?"

"Yes, I did."

"Isn't that highly unusual, Mr. Booth, that you should disdain the use of your chauffeured car and your own state security agents' protection to drive yourself to Camp David, the resort of presidents? Isn't it, Mr. Booth?"

Booth pauses for twenty seconds and doesn't answer.

"That question in order, Governor Booth," states the judge, "and I'd like to know the answer, myself."

"Yes, your honor, several times I have driven to Camp David. I find driving alone a way to get away from the rigors of the confining political life."

"Mr. Booth, when you checked out the shotgun and the jacket, how many orange jackets were in the security post?"

"As I recall, only one."

"Only one!

"You mean of all those jackets, there was only one orange colored jacket?"

"That's right."

"And you were wearing it when the president saw you shoot at him. No more questions, your honor."

"Objection! The prosecutor has made a false statement—in the president's testimony, he said he did not recognize the governor as the man shooting at him or running away," shouts Webb.

"Sustained. Strike that last comment by the prosecutor from the records. Now Mr. Van de Kamp, would you like to put that in the form of a question?" asks the judge.

"Your honor, I have no more questions for this defendant, but I would like to recall the president to the stand for my cross examination, after which the people will be ready to summarize our case."

Judge Wallingsford speaks, "Thank you, Governor Booth, you may step down. The people recall President Morton to the stand and remind him that he is still under oath."

Mokski shams a grin at the president as he stands and strides towards the witness stand.

"Mr. President, I only have a few questions. Sir, previous testimony by your staff has proven that the defendant was not invited to Camp David on March 17, 2011. Do you agree with that testimony ... was the defendant invited?"

"No he wasn't."

"Was the defendant knowledgeable of your habit of taking early morning walks alone on the grounds at Camp David?"

"Yes he was; in fact several times he and I took walks to discuss politics and personal affairs."

"Sir, you stated in your testimony that you heard the first shot and saw leaves falling, and knowing it was meant for you, fell to the ground, only to get up and see a man in an orange jacket fire a second shot. Did you recognize that man as the defendant?"

"No, all I noticed was the orange jacket, and then I fell to the ground as the second shot came over my head."

"So, you did not recognize the man?"

"No I did not."

"Sir, when you stood up after a few seconds, did you recognize the man running away with a shotgun in his hands?"

"Not at the time, but later when the agents brought the man back to the main house, it turned out to be Sandy with handcuffs on. I realized that it was the same man I saw running towards the skeet range."

"Sir, are you saying that the man you saw running away from the agents was indeed the defendant, Governor Sanford Booth?"

"Yes, but—"

"Thank you, Mr. President. I have no further questions, your honor."

The president is in awe; he had more to say on the matter in defense of his friendship and his belief that Sandy could not have attempted such a crime. The prosecutor had not allowed him a chance to state his feelings. Looking at Governor Booth, he feels that he has let him down. The contempt he shows in his features for the prosecutor, however, the jurists and everyone else in the courtroom sees him staring at Governor Booth.

"You may step down, Mr. President; thank you for gracing our courtroom with your presence. Mr. Webb, Mr. Van de Kamp, we are ready for your summations. Are you ready, Mr. Webb?" asks the judge. "Mr. Webb, you are on first."

"Ready, your honor."

President Morton is stepping down from the witness stand. The head bailiff notices the president nearly falling as his right leg had "gone to sleep" and causes him to limp. The bailiff moves to help him and is guiding him to his seat. As the president passes the defense table, he reaches out to shake the hand of Governor Booth. His face shows signs of deep depression, and instead of a handshake, he grabs his chest and falls to the floor. The court is filled with sighs and screams. Secret service agents move to the president's side and others grab the vice president and whisk him out of the courtroom, passing two paramedics coming in through the doorway.

The Resignation

President Morton is resting comfortably in his room at Walter Reed General Hospital. Walking down the hallway towards the room and protected by three agents is Vice President Mokski. A military doctor approaches him.

"What's his condition, Doctor?" asks Mokski.

"The president had a stroke and is recovering nicely," replies the doctor.

"Can I—" Mokski asks, being cut off.

"Yes, you can see him, Mr. Mokski, but only for about five minutes."

"Good, I'll be brief."

Inside the president's room, Mokski is showing him the headlines of the Washington Post which reads, PRESIDENT'S TESTIMONY MOVES JURY. BOOTH GUILTY.

The doctor is in the hallway talking to the agents when he hears Mokski call from within the room.

"Doctor, Doctor! Get in here quick!" He races through the door followed by the agents. Mokski folds the newspaper and places it under his arm. The doctor begins to work feverishly to revive the president, who is having a massive heart attack.

Seated in the president's chair in the Oval Office is Mokski. He is surrounded by the cabinet heads, heads of the FBI and CIA, the joint chiefs of staff and seven Supreme Court justices in robes.

The television monitor is on and tuned in to the 6 o'clock news. The anchorman states, "At 5 o'clock Washington time today, the President of the United States, Richard Morton, resigned. The president, as you know, suffered a massive heart attack and was left with body limb paralysis. The president also cites the failing health of the First Lady and the shocks of three recent assassination attempts on his life as reasons behind his decision to resign. He feels at this time, it would be in the best interest of the country to turn over the reins of the presidency to Vice President James Mokski. That is a summary of the text released through the presidential press secretary from Walter Reed Hospital. Vice president Mokski was sworn in, simultaneous with the resignation, at 5 o'clock today in a brief ceremony at the White House. The oath of office was administered by Chief Justice Barker. And now from the Oval Office is Mokski's first speech as the President of the United States of America."

The News Conference

Mokski pushes back from the table to gain a view of all officials, seemingly looking for reactions to that introduction.

"My fellow citizens. I am saddened as, no doubt you are, by the resignation of our president. I have been close to him, both throughout his candidacy and while we have been serving you in this administration. I feel that we have many challenges ahead of us, and two of the main problems this new administration will face are to balance the budget that was inherited from the previous administrations and ballooned during their eight years in office. You know, when the Dow Jones broke 1500 in December 1985, we Republicans felt, as the investors did, that the interest rates would go down and thereby create opportunities for Congress and Reagan to balance the budget. After G. H. W. Bush left office, interest rates grew, as did inflation. During Bush's term, the Dow Jones grew to 3300 and fell back to the 2200 level. During Clinton's term the DOW grew to over 10,000, the deficit was eliminated, there was a surplus. However, after that God-awful day, September 11th, the economy went to hell in a hand-basket, and many investors lost heavily. Then president G.W. Bush continued his give away of the surplus and created a deficit that threatened Social Security. The feds helped maintain some stability in the economy by lowering interest rates. President Morton and I have found difficulty in dealing with a Democratic Congress, and so it is the same economy today. 'Bush's Wars', as they were called, in Iraq, Iran, and North Korea added over 5 trillion dollars to the deficit. The drastic change in the economy and the wars caused plants to close, unemployment to skyrocket, and our number one social problem, crime, to run rampant The national uproar from all you citizens on the crowded prisons, the recent wholesale release of non-rehabilitated inmates, and, of course, the crime rates are up 1000% in most cities. We've even had vigilante groups that have killed prisoners, jails have been bombed, and just two weeks ago, 140 inmates were killed when the buses they were being transported in were bombed. There is pressure on the federal government to take the burden of the penal system off the backs of the cities, counties, and states. I promise you a new deterrent to crime in the United States. I promise you that this will be accomplished and in doing so, we will balance the budget, balance trade deficits, change economic trends, and turn this country around. As it stands now, $120,000 is the annual figure that it takes to house each of thousands of inmates in our prisons and jails. We will come up with a deterrent that will cut the cost down and cure this problem forever. Healthcare programs for our seniors and lower class citizens have not been approved by Congress. Constitutionally, only prisoners have guaranteed healthcare. But, I guarantee you this, there will be no more dope within the United States borders, no dope dealers, no mafia, no one who will want to rob a bank, commit a crime, steal, rape or kill in this country. For those animals who have the inclination to hurt law-abiding citizens, we plan to change a lot of criminal minds to be do-gooders. We will clean up the backlog in the courts. We will find a way to expediently process all pending trials and appeals. That is why, tonight, I am meeting with the officials you see assembled here. The joint chiefs, cabinet secretaries, FBI, CIA, and the Supreme Court justices. With their cooperation with your new president, we will develop the plan that will make this country all that our forefathers fought to guarantee. Your pursuit of happiness and all that the Constitution provides will be prevalent throughout this land. That is, if you abide by the law of the land and the laws that most of you associate with God in your individual religious affiliations. Thank you."

The Deterrent

The president's press secretary, Ron Baker, turns off the TV monitor. Mokski smiles as he pulls his chair back to the table.

"Gentlemen, effective today, I am declaring war!"

The puzzled faces of the officials look towards the president in awe. He continues.

"Yes, I am declaring war on crime and criminals within the United States, today.

"I've gathered you here today to ask for the same support you gave President Morton, but at a higher cost of your time and service. I will outline a plan with which I will carry through, or which you will carry through in order to expedite its completion. As you can surmise from my speech, from the headlines, and from your own intelligence sources on what's going on in the streets of the cities of this nation, you know that we have a bitter task ahead of us. What I have in outline before you is my plan to establish a deterrent against crime."

The president points to a chart showing the state of Wyoming.

"As you can see, the plan details that we must build one compound for all criminals in the United States. No longer will they be housed in city, county, or state correctional facilities. To the people who act like animals and commit crimes, we will exile them to live off the land or perish. They will be given a chance to prosper as did the early pioneers. Anyone who commits a crime, no matter how minor, will be sent to the compound. I am directing George," referring to George Weitz, the

Secretary of the Interior, whom he points to, "to buy out all residents of the northwest quadrant of the state of Wyoming and to relocate them in 30 days. We will use Yellowstone Park, the Grand Teton Park to Sinks Canyon Park to the south, and Interstate 25 to the east. As you can see, the compound will border Idaho to the West and Montana to the North. You will work with the FBI and the CIA and use their agents as real estate agents. The details of the buyouts are in the package. The premise here is that we are building a military base, and the secrecy of this plan will be at the highest level. Anyone here involved in leaking information about the compound to the press or anyone outside this room will commit an act of treason. Gentlemen, that means that you would spend the rest of your life in the compound. I am directing you, generals, to work together with your Corp of Engineers to construct this compound. We must have the best in security systems that the military and private sectors can provide, including lasers. We must have walls that cannot be scaled to surround that compound. I want an Air Force Base outside the east and west walls and an Army and Marine base on the other two walls. This will add credence to our premise and also provide for helicopter patrols and sonar to detect aircraft that fly over the compound. I want it to be agreed that any aircraft flying under 30,000 feet over the compound is to be escorted out of the area, or shot down, if necessary."

"But, Mr. President," interrupts the Air Force chief, "that area is now under a major route used by commercial airlines, foreign and domestic. We wouldn't want to have a series of Korea 007s."

"Well, General, we'll just have to change those routes, won't we?"

"Yes, sir," sighs the general.

"Continuing, I want the Supreme Court and Congress to pass a law making all crimes punishable by life imprisonment without parole. We will use the powers of this office and the powers of Congress to annex this part of Wyoming to become the prison state. And as the Interior Secretary knows, the majority of that land is already national forest property, including Yellowstone. I will name an individual, shortly, who will head up the new Prison Authority."

The president's plan is to leave all existing buildings within the compound and also crude tools, which inmates might use for construction and farming. The existing water treatment plants and hundreds of fresh water wells will be left intact to provide for that need. There is to be no control of the inmates within the compound. They will have to establish their own order and or government. Medical help will be provided only by inmates with those skills. The plan states that prisoners will be turned out to the elements and will be expected to fend for themselves.

"The jails and courtrooms of this land will be emptied and the only place in these United States where crime will be prevalent will be within the walls of the compound. Gentlemen, I want this program completed twelve months from today. I want you to utilize the private sector with experience in building dams along with the Corp of Engineers in all service branches to meet that deadline. The plans are before you and your individual responsibilities are delineated in detail. I have no doubts that you will maintain the secrecy of this project and carry out your assignments. Thank you, gentlemen, now go to it."

As the officials are picking up their packages and walking out of the Oval Office, Press Secretary Ron Baker whispers to Mokski, "Jim, when this comes off, you will go down as the president of presidents."

The Search

In the visitor's room at the county jail, James Webb is seated in a chair positioned at a long table with stalls. Webb is the only person in the room. A door directly in front of him opens and in walks Sanford Booth. A guard following closely behind him enters and walks over and sits in a chair in the corner of the room. He lights a cigarette while staring at Booth as he sits across from Webb.

"Hello, Governor, how are they treating you, sir?"

The governor's face reflects that he is coping.

"Tell me, James, what are you doing about my appeal?"

"Sir, we're working on that, but having some difficulty in getting the appeal going in the next thirty days as you asked. Look, I've got bad news. You know the agents who were at Camp David and disappeared? Well they were found dead yesterday. They had been shot in the head, gangland style. We're running out of witnesses to corroborate any testimony that a willing witness gives to the judge. Under cross examination and witness protection program, we had a chance with these agents, but not now."

Booth pounds his fist on the table and shakes his head in disgust.

"I understand what you're saying, James; first it was Agent Herman and now these two agents. Have you checked all possibilities and was there anyone else there you can interrogate to determine who was behind framing me or what really happened and how the real assassin escaped the camp? Someone's got to know, and that someone is alive and killing off everyone who knows anything that could free me. I know there was a conspiracy to terminate the president and that I was set up to take the fall."

"I believe that, Governor, but I hope you understand that we are behind you in this tragedy. We are even checking into a lead that Herman was not killed in Iraq, but is in seclusion in Tangier. I have a flight out tomorrow to check it out. But in lieu of any new developments, I still have problems getting the judge to go along with an appeal."

Booth stares at the ceiling and then looks pointedly at Webb. "This place is going to get the best of me. I've got to get out. Out there, I know that I can help you find the truth. But look, Jim, I know that you're doing all you can. Just don't give up on me." Webb shakes his hand suggesting that he will not give up.

"I hope you believe that I'm innocent."

"I do, Governor. I also know that you couldn't have done this to your friend. President Morton knows that too. He is on my list of people to talk to as soon as I learn that his health will allow him to talk about the matter. Maybe he knows more than has been published about the other two attempts on his life. I'm checking out every angle so that I can get this appeal."

"What do you mean when you say that the former President Morton knows?"

"I did talk to him, but did not go too deep because of his condition. He told me that he believes that President Mokski or someone associated with his staff had something to do with all three attempts on his life. And since he is now the president, we have to find and put the loose ends together and see where they lead. Governor, I have to go now, but I'll be in touch as soon as I return from Tangier."

They stand and shake hands, and as they do, the guard jumps up from his chair and seemingly, in one stride in at the governor's side, grabs his arm and says, "That's all, you have to go."

The guard pulls the governor's arm and leads him to the jail door.

The streets and alleys of Tangier are bustling with markets and traders of all wares. Chants of the sellers and buyers fill the air as vigorous trading in underway. Inside a smoke-filled street cellar bar, the sounds of stringed instrument music can be heard. A bearded Agent Herman is seated at a table in a corner of the bar that is closeted with beads hanging from the ceiling. Herman has been drinking heavily and is thoroughly intoxicated. A belly dancer is performing near the hanging beads and opens them to tantalize him by shaking her hips in and out the line of the hanging beads, as if to give him a hip and then take it away in a form of teasing. She approaches his table, places a scarf around his neck and slides it away. Herman pulls the young beauty down onto his lap and tries to kiss her on the mouth through the scarf she wears to hide her face. She forces away from him, but he grabs the end of the scarf around her head. It appears that she pulls him from the table and into the barroom, through the hanging beads, and as her head bends backward, she screams a fearful shriek in her native tongue. The bartender-father cries out, "That's enough, mister, you must leave my daughter—go! She only dances for your pleasure. She is not here to satisfy you. Leave my daughter go!" Herman puts his arms out to reach for the girl, but abruptly drops them to his side, walks back to his chair, sits down, and takes a drink. The girl resumes her dance.

Through the hanging beads that shroud the doorway walks James Webb and Rhashih, a Tangier constable dressed in a white safari suit and wearing a white hat. Webb is similarly attired, with the exception of a white hat. Instead he is wearing dark shades and a replica of a general's cap replete with four stars and crow's nest on the brim. They walk to the bar, sit on stools, and order drinks. The bartender acknowledges them and the presence of the constable with a face full of smiles.

"Yes, Mr. Webb," states Rhashih, "that is the man at that table," pointing a hidden finger towards Herman. "I believe him to be the man you are seeking. He has only been here a short time, but manages to spend money, as you Americans say, like there is no tomorrow. He lives in a rented villa, but comes here each day to drink. Our police have had to take him to the villa several times. In his drunkenness, he has boasted to them that he too was a policeman, a secret service agent for the United States president."

During the conversation, Webb makes eye contact with Herman through the beads.

"Thank you, Constable Rhashih, I'll handle it from here," replies Webb.

They both stand and walk over to the table where Herman is seated. They pull up two chairs from an adjacent table and sit down. Herman looks up at them from his stupor. Webb calls out the name, "Clarence Herman?"

Herman reaches into his jacket and as he does, both Webb and Rhashih are on top of Herman, attempting to wrestle the gun away. Herman manages to free their grips and grabs the belly dancer. He puts the gun to her head and backs to the bar. The bartender pulls a dagger from his sleeve and throws it into Herman's back. Herman falls on top of the dancer to the floor. Webb and Rhashih rush to his side. Together, they lift him off the girl, who gets up and runs into the embrace of her father around the bar. They drag Herman to an area on the floor where the sunlight through a ceiling window makes a spotlight on the floor. Gasping for air and near death, Herman asks, "You're that attorney, Webb, how did you find me? They told me no one would ever find me."

"They who?" asks Webb. Herman's eyes roll upward.

"Look, Herman, you're not going to make it, and an innocent governor is paying for a crime that you know the truth about. Tell me what you know about that day at Camp David."

Herman gasps for air again and his body convulses.

"It was Mokski, the VP. He tried to assassinate the president three times and it didn't work. Booth got in the way." Herman coughs. "But when I heard about the other agents being snuffed out, I didn't feel safe even though I was here. I figured my time was any day. It's too bad that I won't be going back to help you nail that bastard. Oh-h!" cries Herman, as he succumbs.

The Prison Authority

Webb's commercial airliner from Tangier lands at Reagan National Airport. Two of the president's secret service agents board the plane before passengers are allowed to disembark. They approach Webb and tell him they are there to escort him to the president, who wants to have a conference.

In the oval office, Mokski is with Baker, and a female voice comes over the intercom and announces, "James Webb is here, Mr. President."

"Tell him to come in," voices the president. Webb enters the oval office and Mokski looks him over and asks, "So what were you doing in Tangier, James?"

"Sir, I went there to check out rumors that could help my client, Governor Booth."

"Well, James, tell me, did you find anything?"

Webb pauses and then states, "No, the rumor did not check out, seems that the party had become a drunkard and was killed in a bar."

Mokski looks at Baker and smiles. He stands and walks around the desk to where Webb is standing, gains eye contact with him, and says, "You should give up the search. Stop wasting your time. No one can be freed after being convicted as a presidential assassin. Besides, your time will become limited. I know you are a resourceful person. And you're not a quitter. I called you here to ask you to become a member of my cabinet."

Webb blushes. Never in his life had he dreamed of such a high post. Everyone wants to be president, but realistically, a cabinet post is not as easy to get.

"Baker, here, will fill you in on all the details. I expect you to get back to me tomorrow with your answer. I've got a lot of confidence in your past experiences, so I expect an affirmative answer. Ron, make sure you remind Mr. Webb that this is top secret and of the consequences if he should reveal it. Thank you, gentlemen, that'll be all."

Webb and Baker walk out of the oval office. Mokski walks over to his desk and picks up a telephone. He calls someone named Carter. "Carter, Mokski here. You know that Tangier connection. I want it eliminated. Get back to me to confirm when handled."

In the visitor room of the county jail, Webb is again seated across the table. Booth and the same guard enter and follow the same procedure.

"Governor," whispers Webb, "we were right. Herman was alive, but I saw him killed in Tangier. Before he died, he linked President Mokski to the three attempts on President Morton. He told me that you were caught in the middle and used as a scapegoat. In other words, they had planned to frame you no matter how the attempt turned out. I learned that Herman had been given money to buy his silence and to keep him in exile. He had obviously gone to Tangier on his own, after hearing about the killing of one of his agents."

All ears, Booth interrupts, "But, James, now we have a problem— Herman cannot not testify, and we don't know if he would have had you brought him back alive. You have got to get this information to Judge Wallingsford and bring up the new developments. I'm sure he'll listen now and grant me an appeal. The mere fact that the agencies covered up with the first lie that Herman had been killed in Iraq should warrant an appeal."

"I'll do it," Webb reluctantly agrees. "I'm on my way to the judge's house, but don't get your hopes up. He may be tied to Mokski, who has recommended his appointment to the Supreme Court. This is not the same as Watergate, and he may not want to rock the boat."

They both stand. Booth's lifted spirits are noticeable as he waves goodbye and snaps his fingers to indicate to the guard that he is ready to go back to his cell. As quickly as the door closes behind Webb, it opens again and Webb comes back into the room.

"Guard," he calls, "can we have a few minutes more?"

The guard nods and sits down on his chair. Webb and Booth stand across the table.

"Governor, I forgot to tell you. There is something very important going on and it may have an impact on you. The whole state of Wyoming is in uproar, and the whole country for that matter. The government has exercised eminent domain over the northwest quadrant of Wyoming to build what they say are military bases. They are buying property and relocating every person in that region. Mokski has asked me to join his cabinet. I believe that I will accept. To be close to him might provide me an opportunity to learn more about your predicament. Maybe I can learn the damaging evidence needed to get you acquitted. I can tell you only one thing ... I have got to get you out of here before that project in Wyoming is completed. I'll see you, Governor. God Bless."

Booth notices a dejected look on the face of Webb as he walks out of the door.

Twelve months have passed. During that time, Webb has contacted Judge Wallingsford, who wanted more proof that Herman was actually killed in Tangier. Webb attempted to get the remains of Herman through Rhashih, but only learned that the body had disappeared from the morgue. Judge Wallingsford had been approved by Congress to become a Justice and no longer had responsibility for the Governor's case. Webb assumed his new role as head of the Prison Authority and directs the final construction phase.

The Compound

In Wyoming, final inspection is underway. Mokski had been stockpiling materials and equipment for months prior to him becoming president. The massive task force was able to build the compound in record time. The slowest part was waiting for the concrete to harden. Walls have been built and there are four tunnels at each corner of the compound. Laser beams have been tested and proven to be effective in eradicating anything or anyone attempting to cross the walls. A satellite fleet is in place and monitors all of the ground area in the compound— satellites that are armed and can thwart an escape attempt with lasers from the heavens. Military bases have been set up outside each wall. Webb is on the scene and has been spending all of his time on this project and none on the appeal for Booth.

A State van pulls up in front of Attica prison. There are eight prisoners inside, including Governor Booth. He has been transferred here for incarceration. Booth walks down the hallways. Each cell is packed to overflowing with inmates. Newspaper and TV news had reported this phenomenon for the past year. The noise of gates slamming behind him as he goes from cellblock to cellblock is heard and leaves him with a feeling of finality. Booth and the other seven inmates are placed in a holding tank with twenty who were already there. Inmates shout obscenities to the new arrivals. One states to the governor's attention, "Hey, who's going to be my lady? Hey, maybe that pretty one in front."

He is indicating the governor, who strides out in front of the group as he enters the holding tank. It is common knowledge that inmates are held here until assigned to a cellblock.

A Mexican inmate, with his shirt unbuttoned, shows his muscular upper body and with a bandanna tied around his bushy, dark hair, walks up to the governor and stares into his eyes, nearly nose to nose and breath to breath, as he back peddles while Booth keeps walking. The handsome Booth stands 6-foot-3, and about five inches taller than the Mexican. Booth had planned to show no fear or to be intimidated by an inmate, so almost instinctively, he pushes the Mexican to the floor and walks over him. The inmate grabs his legs and a fight ensues with three other inmates joining in to help the Mexican. They are beating Booth about the head and kicking him. From out of the group of inmates who were there previously comes a 6-foot-6 black American named Lewis, who pulls the foes off the governor, strikes blows to two of them, and the other two back away. Lewis' authority level as the superior inmate shows through the fear in the faces of the four inmates as they cringe against the walls.

Booth is unconscious as Lewis kneels down beside his body, shakes Booth's head, and as he comes to and looks into Lewis's piercing eyes and hardened face, he passes out again.

In the exercise yard the very next day, Booth is walking through the yard minding his own business. He sees the Mexican who had jumped him with the other three inmates walking towards him. Lewis steps between and they turn abruptly and walk away. Lewis approaches the governor, and in a deep voice says to him, "You are a lucky son of a bitch."

Booth looks up at Lewis and thankfully says, "I appreciate what you did for me, but I can take care of myself."

"Look, white boy, I just came here, but I've been here before and everyone knows that I'm boss here. You just stay in line, and I'll take care of you. Don't cross me. You understand that, boy?"

Booth nods his head, indicating to Lewis that he understands. Booth is grateful that Lewis has befriended him, because he had learned earlier that to be accepted by the dominant inmates was assurance of survival, even if it meant doing special favors for them and of course, to be strong and not allow them to turn him into a punk.

Almost simultaneously, the alarm sounds, ending the exercise period. Inmates quizzically look up to the guards on the walls, because it is only 2 p.m. and the exercise period always ends at 4 p.m. Lockdown is enforced as all inmates are placed in cellblocks. Needless to say, none of them know that the President of the U. S. has given the order that all prisoners in jails and prisons all over the country be locked up and radio and TV privileges be taken away for the balance of that day. This is due to the News conference that the president is to give at 6 p.m. Eastern time.

The Address

In the East Room of the White House, Presidential Secretary Baker walks up to the podium and addresses the group of TV, radio, and newspaper press.

"Gentlemen and ladies, would you please be seated. I'd like to alert the networks that within ten seconds, the president will be here."

The reporters take their seats. The room is filled to capacity. In the previous news conferences Mokski had handpicked reporters, but today they were allowed to enter on a first come-first enter basis.

Baker announces, "Gentlemen and ladies, the President of the United States."

Mokski walks up to the podium.

"Fellow citizens, press, law-abiding citizens, and citizens who wish to commit crimes. I have messages for both of the latter groups. First, the law abiders. After this day, no longer will you have to be fearful or have to worry about crimes being committed against you or anyone else, nor will you worry about muggers, burglars, or murderers. We, as promised, have in the last twelve months created the world's greatest deterrent to crime. And you, the law-abiding citizens, will benefit from the efforts of your president and your government from this day forward. To those who wish to commit crimes and those who are imprisoned at this moment, your government will no longer use your taxpayers' dollars to support prisons and jails as you now know them to be. We created the ultimate prison: the compound. We feel that all who have committed crimes and who do so in the future should be returned to the elements, whereby they will fend for themselves, just like our forefathers who lived off the land and made a life for themselves. And all you activists who believe this to be inhumane treatment of our prisoners should consider the inhumane acts that they have perpetrated against mankind. Inhumane crimes deserve inhumane punishment. Although, I must state that prisoners will have freedom within the compound. We are giving them an opportunity to build a new society between the walls of the compound. The day will come when the only crimes committed in these United States will be the crimes committed by prisoners against prisoners within the walls of the compound.

Yes, it has been reported that what we were building in the state of Wyoming is a military fortress. No, that is not correct. What has been built is the most sophisticated compound for prisoners that could ever be conceived. The greatest minds of science and engineering in this world have collaborated in record time to create the safeguards and deterrents that you will see later when we reveal to the world our deterrent to crime. There is no way to escape. No way to enter unless the government puts someone in there. There is no exit unless it's because of death and your family wants the body."

While the president is speaking, a video tape of the compound is shown on a screen to his left.

"Now you will not see all of the security measures that have been employed. The only ones who will learn about the deterrent will be those prisoners who try to escape or anyone who tries to enter via the walls. It does have strategically located tunnels that food will initially be shipped in, and where fail safe door lock systems will be operative. We have left all buildings for shelter, added some farm equipment, mules, water treatment plants for the inmates' use in order to survive within the compound. This, to the prisoners, could be "hell on earth" or it could be a new start if they choose leaders who organize and utilize skills that some had before they committed their crimes. No law enforcement will be provided inside. They will have to establish their own order. Medical supplies will be provided for use by those prisoners with the skills to administer medical help, if they choose to. They will be commingled with murderers, rapists, thieves, prostitutes, white collar criminals, and drug offenders. Those citizens who commit the least of crimes, from stealing a loaf of bread to murder, will immediately be tried and sent to the compound on proof of guilt. No more will citizens think about committing a crime against their fellow man. Your constitutional rights will be enhanced. Our savings on prisons, county jails, and related rehabilitation facilities will have a monetary effect that will balance the federal budget. Savings in the courts, expensive trials, judges, and even lawyers will have to practice in other fields. We predict that the need for representation in criminal cases will diminish by 99 percent. It is very important that everyone within the sound of my voice pass the word that: 'Crime will never pay … in the USA … beginning today.'

"I want to wrap this up by letting you know that your Supreme Court and your Congress have passed law that any crime committed in these United States of America and its territories is punishable by life imprisonment with no parole. I must repeat that. Effective today, the laws of this country provide for life imprisonment without parole for any crime committed. All prisoners of lesser defined crimes will have their sentences reviewed by wardens or local jail authorities and some will be released. All long-term felons, murderers, thieves, drug offenders, and habitual criminals will be transferred to the compound. In fact, at this very hour, these procedures are being acted on and the first groups of prisoners are on their way to the Deterrent.

"I am sending a 'special warning' to the dope pushers, the mobsters, and organized crime within our borders. Your efforts to commit crimes and perpetuate sickness amongst our children with dope had better cease. No longer will we tolerate this activity within the confines of the United States. Turn your dirty money into responsible and productive businesses that will affect the future of this country, less you find yourselves in the compound."

Webb walks to the podium and stands beside the president.

"Our prison authority is headed up by the man who stands next to me, Mr. James Webb. Together with the CIA, FBI, and our military, the prison authority will seek out and find all those in the mafia who seek

41

to perpetuate those crimes you are carrying on at this very moment and we will see you go into the compound. We are asking every citizen, good or bad, to turn over a new leaf today and walk a straight path. The path that Americans have fought and died for. As I stated earlier, your constitutional rights will be enhanced by this Act. In conclusion, I wish to say that 'Crime will never pay … in the USA … beginning today.'

"Now if there are any questions?"

The reporters are stunned and in awe of Mokski. None of them speak up. As the president gazes about the audience, he asks again.

"Are there any questions? If not, then take this to your readers and viewers, 'Crime will not pay, in the USA, beginning today.' Thank You."

As the president walks away from the podium towards the exit, the reporters stand in reverence to this powerful speech. Applause, by a few, slowly comes to clapping by all present. Mokski stops, turns around and acknowledges with a salute.

The reporters all break for the doors to report on the speech and the new reformation of the U.S. on crime to their newspapers and networks.

The Transfer to the Compound

The compound borders on the east wall along the Wyoming, Montana, and Idaho border, down to Niobrara County at the southern wall north of the North Platte River through the counties of Converse to Fremont to the west wall built on Interstate 25, and from Sinks Canyon State Park to the south up to Yellowstone National Park and Montana border where the north wall extends to the east wall.

Prisoners are arriving at the compound. At the air bases, planes are offloading thousands of inmates from all over the states. Buses are completing the last leg of the transfer by dropping them off at the tunnel gates. At the tunnel entrances, instructions and advice is being given to them over a PA system. The information tells them where to find cities, water sources, where to look for food supplies, tools, and winter clothing. The announcer encourages them to take advantage of their freedom to start over, live off the land, and to choose leaders in order that they work together.

Survival kits given to each inmate include comb, tooth brush and paste, soap, first aid kit, and an assortment of perennial vegetable seed packets. There are announcers at each of the four tunnels. Armed military line the path from the buses to the tunnel entrance. Some break the line and charge the guards. Some are pushed back and a few break through the defense line. Guards shoot them with Taser rifles and return them to the line entering the tunnels. Prisoners enter the tunnel into the compound. Hundreds at first, then thousands mill around the tunnel, not wanting to venture out into the compound. Some look to see if they are really void of guards. After the realization that they are free hits them, they run without stopping until they can no longer be seen by the reluctant ones still at the tunnel.

Inside a military transport filled with prisoners, Booth is seated between Lewis and John French, a former policeman committed for accepting bribes and the one person who has recognized the governor and has told all the other cell mates. "We will have to take charge of those who follow us," Booth speaks. "I've got a map of Wyoming that the pilot gave me, heck if I know why he singled me out. But look here, it's like he's trying to tell me something. This area is circled, so we should think about settling in Yellowstone Park. There we will take control in order to survive. Many will head to the southern borders where the climate is better year round."

A feeble looking inmate across the aisle from Booth stands up out of the hammock-like seat and screams, "I'm not going to go, I won't go, I won't go!"

He goes to his knees and bangs his head on an exposed metal beam. He bangs his head so severely that his skull cracks open and his brain ejaculates adrenalin all over the ceiling of the airplane. He falls to the floor and dies. None of the inmates or the 4 guards at each end of the plane move to his position on the floor. One guard at the rear of the plane starts to walk and the other pulls his shirt and tells him, "Stay here. You go into the middle of these animals and they'll tear you to shreds. Leave him be."

The guard shakes his head and steps back.

Lewis, looking at the dead man, says to Booth, "You will see a lot more of that, especially when these fools, who can't fend for themselves, are on their own."

Booth replies, "I'm glad you understand that fact, which is why we have to establish some kind of order, a brotherhood, once we get there to avoid a chaotic situation."

"A kay-wut?" asks Lewis, "I can't understand you lawyers."

"You understand B-A-D, don't you? A bad situation to you, Lewis," smiles Booth.

Their transport lands and taxis at the air base near the northwest tunnel. The inmates begin to deplane. While walking towards the front, Booth notices a row of women inmates. Some look haggard and others look well kept. His eyes catch those of a red-haired woman in her twenties. They smile. Lewis notices their contact and jokes, "Sisterhood too?"

As they exit the plane, the buses are waiting. On board the bus, Booth manages to talk a female inmate into moving across the aisle and he sits next to the redhead.

"How do you feel about taking this safari?"

She turns her head to the window and doesn't speak.

"Oh, so you're going to ignore me. Well, that's your right. You'll have plenty of time where we going. Time to speak or not to."

"Going to take a little, little journey, Going to take a—"

In his deep baritone, Lewis sings and stops when he hears the guard at the front of the bus yell, "Be quiet back there!"

As they unload, Booth reads the sign high over the entrance which states "Tunnel # ONE." Booth, French, Lewis, and Lewis' gay slave lurching behind him are in the middle of the lines. The PA announcer is again explaining how to get to the cities and giving advice.

Booth recognizes the voice, and as he draws near the PA stage, he moves from the group and calls out, "Webb! James Webb!"

Webb sees Booth and replies, "Governor?"

He hands the mike to the regular announcer, who puts down his sandwich and continues. Webb moves through the guards and walks over to Booth and shakes his hand.

"What happened, James? I haven't heard from you for months," asks Booth, as he grips Webb's hand tightly and places his other hand on his elbow.

Webb grimaces as he feels the pain, but replies, "Governor, I've been working on this project for the president, and even though you are going into the compound, I still have hope for your release. Governor, I want you to stay in Yellowstone Park and keep in touch. The only way this can happen is for you to be the inmates' contact with the outside, the government. I'm here because I knew when you would arrive. I want to tell the inmates that you will be the only contact with the outside. Hopefully that will help protect you. Will you agree, Governor?"

Booth loosens his grip, looks backs towards the inmates, turns to Webb, and nods his head affirmatively. Webb then takes him by the arm and leads him to the stage.

"So it was you who had the pilot give me the map."

"Yes, sir," smiles Webb.

The inmates all stop walking and stand looking towards the stage in awe. The guards' reaction is about the same, as they focus their attention on the stage instead of the prisoners.

Upon reaching the microphone, Webb tells the prisoners that Booth is to be their only contact with the outside and they should take care to see that he is protected. Further, he tells them that monthly, Booth will meet with officials in the security tunnel to seek help with their needs, problems, medical situations, or other important emergencies.

Finally, he says, "I have every confidence in the governor, and you must trust him to represent you whenever we meet in the future months. Spread the word to others who have entered before you as you travel through the compound. We will tell those who are to follow. That is all. Proceed to the tunnel."

The guards gesture for the inmates to resume their walk towards the tunnel. As they are walking off the stage, Webb tells Booth that in this way he will be able to keep in touch.

"I plan to follow through with my investigation and get your freedom. Mokski trusts me now that I hold one of his cabinet posts. I am so close to him that I shudder at the things I have learned. And I know he will slip one day and open the bag on the President Morton affair."

"You know what, James, I believe you," he says as he walks briskly to join the other inmates.

Upon clearing the tunnel to the interior of the compound, Booth finds Lewis, French, and hundreds of inmates waiting off to the side, while others run and walk southerly towards the cities.

"Once a governor, now a warden. So how does it feel, Warden?" smiles French.

"Let's forget about the governor and the warden bit. You know what our plans are, so let's go," Booth says, speaking directly to Lewis and French.

He raises his voice to the others and tells them, "The best weather is to the south, where they are headed," pointing to the inmates moving south, "but any of you men and women who want to follow us, we're head northwest. Pick up your backpacks because we're leaving right now. Good luck to those of you moving to the south; if you need us, we'll be in Yellowstone Park."

The groups disperse in all directions and even though inmates, they smile and enjoy their freedom.

The Park Life

It had been a rough journey for the group that had arrived at the abandoned Yellowstone Inn in Yellowstone Park. Numerous stragglers were left behind because of injuries. Others took refuge in small towns along the way. Two others were killed in fights over who would occupy farms. Booth and his cohorts did not get involved in settling the disputes or in any punishment for the killers. They ignored the problems and continued their journey.

More than 2000 in all had made it to the park. A small number considering the fact that over 670,000 inmates would initially be introduced into the penal compound colony.

Booth spoke to the gathering, "I will house in this old historic inn. There are cabins scattered throughout these mountains and abandoned businesses and homes at the bottom of it. Tomorrow we will divide up into search parties and locate everyone on their own parcel. You have been given pencil and papers; I want each of you to write down your skills. I hope we can all work together to functionally set up a community. We are especially interested in medical, construction, farming, and mechanical experience."

That night they gather around a bonfire and Booth breaks them up into groups of 50 to 100. He has each of the inmates introduce themselves and tell of their skills. He learns that there is a mix of all important occupations he forecasted as needed to build communities.

The Telecast

It is a cold, dreary Saturday morning in Washington. Mokski and his press secretary are meeting with Webb to discuss the successful transfer of all prisoners to the compound.

"You know what gave me the idea was the fact that in Colonial days what is now the state of Georgia was a penal colony. Of course, it was controlled." Mokski told them that he wanted film made of the inmates and specifically he wanted only the bad things on film. "Murders, defiant ones, fights, hunger, escape attempts to show the power of the lasers; all these and more do I want on film. I want it shown on all the networks and independent stations, cable and satellite at this time, 1 p.m., every Saturday. I want the world to stop at one o'clock, when I expect everyone to be watching. This in itself will act as a deterrent for those contemplating crime. I want all the gross details on film, and I want the first film in three weeks."

Baker interrupts, "Do you propose we send film crews into the compound, and if so, how do we protect them?"

"I see no problem with that. We can send in ten SWAT teams or a company of military and film near the tunnels or you can even go to Hollywood. I'm joking of course," he laughs.

"Baker, you have the connections—you make all the arrangements, and I'll provide the security," states Webb.

"I'll be setting up the first council meeting with the compound representative."

"I hear you chose Booth to represent the inmates, Webb. Why that choice?" asks Mokski.

"Sir, I know he is capable, and if anyone can bring peace and harmony amongst those prisoners, he has the best chance."

"Yeah, I guess you're right, if he lives long enough." Mokski replies. "It's too bad about his situation. I thought about pardoning him a couple of months ago."

"Is that still a possibility?" Webb asks in a sudden burst of enthusiasm.

"Not now," Mokski replies "The law now states the only way anyone leaves the compound is through death, that is, if the family wants the remains."

Webb thinks to himself, *Now why would he even think about a pardon?*

Saturday arrives, and at 1 p.m., ninety percent of the population is glued to the television. Traffic is non-existent. Even lighter than Super Bowl Sunday or in the sixties when President Kennedy was interred. James Webb is in his office preparing for his meeting with Booth. He ponders the finality of the new law that prevents Booth from leaving the compound even if he were cleared. Of course, to clear him would mean having Mokski indicted. An even tougher choice, no matter what the evidence, since he has taken control and promises a better life without crime, no deficits, and lower taxes. *And the citizens are actually liking these new changes,* he ponders.

Webb looks at his watch and turns on the TV set on the bookshelf opposite his desk.

The program comes on the screen at exactly 1 p.m. The announcer is Press Secretary Baker.

"Citizens of the United States of America, this is the first of mandatory viewing of the life and times in the compound. Since our president stated 'That crime will not pay in the USA,' all prisons and jails have been emptied and all inmates are now in the compound. There have been reports of some inmates taking advantage of their new start and they are farming the land, but the majority of our reports are as you will be seeing in the next few minutes—violence, violence and violence. We have filmed inmates who remain in the northern part and are dying from weather exposure. Some have attempted escape and have paid the price. We have also interviewed some of the inmates on their first three weeks in the compound. You will hear and see their reactions. These interviews speak for themselves."

The film shows a snaggle-toothed black man exhorting that he will rape all white women who are sent to the compound. Other blacks say they will steal food and take shelter away from all weaklings. Burly whites, exhorting they are no better, and they have and will continue to rape, white, black, Mexican, Oriental, and old women, as well as young boys.

"If they don't fit in, they die."

"We kill here."

"There is no punishment for crime here."

"This is Hell on earth."

As different inmates take turns speaking and waving the "F" finger at the camera, other men and women whose dress is deplorable are crying to their relatives at home.

"All I did was rob a gas station!"

"Pray that I die; there is no other way to get out."

Others exhort lesser crimes and plead for their families to change this form of sentencing. One muscle-bound inmate walks briskly toward the camera and the cameraman moves backward until he stops. He shouts, "Come on down! We'll send you home in a box, if you're lucky. I am king here! I am the boss! These people do as I say. I am KING-G-G!"

And simultaneously a scrawny man clubs him to death on camera, takes his spot in front of the camera, and beats his bony chest.

"Now for prisoners who have already tried the deterrents—that is, they tried to escape," announces Baker.

The film shows lasers cutting down inmates within 100 yards of the wall.

Click! Webb turns off the TV.

"That's enough," he talks out loud, and he sits down to complete the preparation for his meeting on the 1st with Booth.

The Tunnel

Booth hadn't remembered much about the tunnel when he entered the compound weeks ago. The doors were wide open to allow large groups of inmates to pass through. He did remember that it was an elaborate facility. As he stood outside the tunnel, a deep voice comes over a speaker and asks, "Identify yourself and for what reason do you approach this tunnel?"

"I am Sanford Booth, the inmate representative here to confer with Mr. James Webb," he replies.

"Approach the door, Booth, and do not touch any doors or walls as you proceed, and wait for each door to open. Should you touch anything other than the floor you walk on, you will die from electrical shock or you will activate lasers that will cut you in half."

Apprehensive, Booth lingers outside the first door. Once inside the first room, he sees the elaborate maze. Concrete partitions about five feet high and each studded with electronic devices, which he assures himself to be the lasers that the voice has referenced. Beyond the maze is a six-foot-wide sliding steel door. Suddenly the door behind him slams shut, lights dim to darkness and a buzzing sound permeates and brings on a myriad of greenish-yellow laser lines meeting at more than fifty points and crossing in numerous directions throughout the room.

"Do not move, Booth," the voice commands.

"I will direct you on every step and every movement. Pay close attention, because since you are the first to have the privilege of coming through the tunnel, it's as new for me as it is for you.

Booth yells, "And I have to put my life in your hands? Hey, I want out of here. Open the door and let me go back."

"Sorry, Booth, that door behind you will not open until you have successfully made it through the tunnel. If I open it now, you die," the voice responds.

"Well, then I'll stay right here until you figure out how to change this damn thing so I can leave."

"Well, Booth, I hope you can stay awake for the rest of your life and stand on two feet, because the moment you touch the floor with a third part of your body, you will die. Remember, either way, you will come through, dead or alive."

A bank of laser beams in front of him disappear.

"Walk forward to the opening in front of you."

Booth follows the voice commands.

"Stop."

Another bank of beams disappear in front of him as those in the back of him reappear.

Booth hears the buzzing sound and looks behind to see the beams. The voice leads him through this stop and start procedure within the maze and past the steel door until he ends up where he began. He had seen no opening to reach the steel doors in front as he passed it.

"Stop and turn around slowly," the voice instructs.

"Now the lights are coming on and you will repeat the trip you just made, but you won't see the lasers. I hope you follow my instructions for each opening because you won't get any other but this one, start!"

Booth is unaware that the power of the lasers has been turned down to no more than a sting. He moves towards the first opening and stops until he hears the buzzing sound in front of him diminish. He proceeds through three openings without a hitch, quizzically, but hoping that he makes the right choices and all the time talking and cursing the voice for playing games with his life. Now in the middle he stands before two openings, which both appear to lead to the steel door. He waits for the buzzing sound to diminish. Confused, he chooses the opening to his right and is struck by the shock from a beam on his right arm which he waves in front as he nears the opening. Squatting down, he looks at his arm to see if it's still there. Standing, he shouts, "Let me out of here. I don't have to go through this. To hell with the meeting. Let me out!"

The lights dim to darkness once more and all the beams reappear. The opening to his left is clear. He collects himself and starts through the maze until he reaches the steel door in front. A four-foot-wide section drops on a track into the floor, revealing more steel, but beams buzz between the openings where the section was. The steel doors open to reveal a long tunnel and simultaneously, the beams in front of him fade out.

"Proceed through the tunnel, Booth. You made it, so far."

Webb is seated in an office viewing Booth's movements on a video screen. Booth is walking through the tunnel, being careful to stay in the middle away from the beams on each wall. He comes to another steel door that opens into a central room where he is met by armed guards who make him turn around and begin to frisk his body for hidden weapons. Getting an "all clear," two of the guards lead him by the arms towards the office where Webb is waiting.

"Where is the son of a bitch with the voice?" asks Booth of the guards. One replies, "He's in here."

Booth could see no one but the guards and figured it was probably the one who was chuckling. In the center of the room is a bank of master computer mainframes, and on a far wall, two analysts are working with several terminals. The door to the office is open and Webb meets him there and shakes his hand.

"Governor, it's good to see you looking so well. I've heard and seen how tough things are in there. Come, sit down."

"Why?" Booth asks, "Why?"

"Why what, governor?" Webb responds.

"Why did you have me go through that tormenting?"

"It could have been worse, Governor. I asked that the lasers be turned down to a mere shock. That's why you still have your arm intact."

Booth feels his arm and looks at Webb.

"We want you to tell the inmates that there is no way out. Believe me, the lasers will dissect and dismember body parts for anyone we don't want to enter."

"You've convinced me, James," he says sarcastically. "Makes me feel good to know that you are still on my side."

"Governor, tell me about the compound and what I can do to help you. I've seen films of the atrocities that are prevalent in the southern sector, and each time I look to see if you are in any of the groups that have been filmed."

"What kind of atrocities are you talking about, James? We only have knowledge of some infighting near the southern walls and in the central sector, but for the most part, that's no different than when the inmates were in cells."

Webb describes the account of the Saturday telecasts.

"I'll check that out when I get back and report to you next month. In the meantime, here is a list of items we need. The most important is the medical supplies. Now, I hope you haven't given up on finding the true assassin. Find Gloria Young, my secretary. I know that she is the key. I can't imagine why, but I feel it."

Standing and ready to leave, he says, "Do that for me, and next time maybe you'll have more to report on Mokski and I'll have more to tell you about the compound."

Booth's trip back through the first tunnel door was not as traumatic as the trip coming in. Walking through the central room, he states to the guards, "You son of a bitch, whichever one you are, don't play with me on the way out!"

As he reaches the first door, a voice comes from the master computers in the middle of the room, saying, "Have a good trip back, Booth."

He looks with wide eyes at the computer as two guards lead him into the tunnel.

Through the maze, power is being shut down twenty feet to their front and on again behind them as they take each step. They dare not stop because the sequence would not. Booth exits the final door to the compound and does not look back, but hears the sound of doors closing and lockup as he heads towards Yellowstone.

The Missing Link

Al Harley's Place is a nightclub in Los Angeles featuring mud wrestling women. This swank club in the Westwood district is frequented by FBI agents from the nearby office in West Los Angeles. Robert Jinx is a treasury agent with previous service in the Washington, DC, area. Jinx had lived next door to Webb and kept up with his former neighbor's defense of Sanford Booth. Jinx's eyes are focused on a blonde mud wrestler. Three other agents are seated at the table with him.

"I know that blonde from somewhere," he utters.

"I thought you said that you've never been here, Bob?" asks the curly headed agent.

"I haven't, I mean, I met her somewhere, but not as a wrestler. I just can't place her."

Jinx walks over to the bar, gets the attention of one of the busy bartenders and asks, "Tell me, what is the name of the blonde wrestler?"

"Babette," he replies, "but there is no fraternizing allowed."

"No, that's her stage name, what's her real name?"

"I just tend bar, mister. That's the only name I know. If a girl says her name is 'Gypsy Rose Lee,' we believe her and don't ask questions. Now, can I get you a cocktail?"

"No thanks," answers Jinx, staring at the girl on stage as he walks back to the table.

"Well, Mr. Super Agent, did you find out how you know her?" asks his agent friend.

"No, but I don't forget a face, it'll come to me."

The blonde wrestler completes her win, leaves the main room, and goes behind curtains.

The Organizing

At the campfire that night, Booth tells of his experience going through the tunnel. Only sound other than his voice is the crackling of the wood in the four-foot-high campfire that lights up the faces of the inmates. The amber glow shows different degrees of astonishment, disbelief, fear, and even adventuresome looks. Booth spots the face of the redhead when the flames cause her face to glow, and her beauty captivates him, causing him to pause and stare. Booth warns those who have ideas of attempting to escape through the tunnels or over the walls that such an attempt would surely be fatal. He asks how the groups are progressing with their plans. Communications group leader, Red Johnson, a former computer programmer who was jailed for fleecing funds from a bank, tells how he has pieced together parts and made a ham radio. The compound walls have jamming devices to restrict signals going into the compound; however, safeguards had not set up to restrict signals going out. Red tells how his group is close to finishing work on a satellite dish that would override the jamming devices and pick up TV and radio signals. Since signals are restricted coming in, they would have a scramble-free system. There are seven farmers in the group at Yellowstone, who were jailed for either murder of bank managers or theft after their farms were auctioned off during the agriculture crisis. Johnny Brownlee heads that group and tells of the tools that were left behind at the park. He plans to organize the entire camp to get involved in cultivating prime farmland in the flats below the park. Corn, potatoes, and wheat would be the main crops. All other vegetables seeds would be planted in parcels near the cabins and on the park grounds. He tells of how they will have to become a vegetarian society in order to survive. Meat would be available as soon as they made bow and arrows and built traps to catch buffalo, deer, elk, moose, and rabbits, which are plentiful in the hills surrounding the park.

Booth takes a seat next to the redhead. She looks him in the eyes and states, "I ignored you once, but at that time, I didn't want to trust anyone. I was scared and still am."

"What's your name?' he asks.

"Jessica Hill," she replies.

"Oh, after Martha, you're the second famous lady who says she's innocent of being charged with embezzlement at that stock brokerage firm."

"It's true. I was in the wrong place at the right time for my bosses, who had knowledge that I knew too much about their insider trading deals. I didn't have a fair trial."

"Join the group," Booth interjects.

"I know about you," Jessica smiles. "You're the main one in here who should be here. Trying to kill the president is the worst crime of all. I don't understand why you were made the contact for us with the government."

"Perhaps my being innocent might have something to do with that choice."

She stares at Booth as he is listening attentively to the group leaders telling of their plans to organize the park. She thinks, *Maybe he's telling the truth. He's so handsome.* Booth looks at her while she is having this thought and she manages a smile that causes him to smile back.

"Can I walk you back to your cabin after this meeting is over?" he asks.

She looks down to the ground where she is scratching drawings in the dirt.

"OK," she scratches in the dirt and points to it.

Booth goes near the fire and tells the group to meet in the morning to get started on the plans. They walk to Jessica's cabin, which to Booth's surprise is down the hill below the inn where he lives. She and two other women are sharing the housing. There haven't been any problems with rape or molesting women at the park. Some men and women have coupled up and others have stuck with their own sex, like Jessica and her roommates.

The cabin has a porch, small living area, bedroom with two queen beds, and a kitchenette. Plumbing in the bathroom is inoperative until one of the crews is able to get the pumping station going again. Latrines have been dug near each inn.

"I guess you expect me to invite you in and sleep with you," she says as she looks up at him.

"Not so. I haven't slept with a woman in four years."

"What about your wife, weren't you sleeping with her?"

"June died four years ago. And why bring up sex? Is that all you have on your mind, what with AIDS in the prison system?"

"No, I just assumed that you … well, you're in charge, and why are you singling me out? There are 400 other women in this camp. I sort of thought you were exercising your privileges, being top man and all."

"Look, I don't know why I singled you out, except for the red hair. June had—"

She cuts him off. "So that's it. I remind you of your dead wife. I imagine that is about the most honest come on that any man up here can have. So what do we do now?"

"I guess we sleep together," grins Booth.

Inside the cabin, Jessica is nude and Booth is in his shorts. She walks up to him and he embraces and kisses her passionately.

"Still remind you of your wife?" she asks.

"Yeah."

"At least you're honest about this. Did she kiss you like this?"

Jessica mouths a lasting, tongue-lashing kiss.

"Whoa!" Booth gasps for air. "Keep that up and it won't be long before I—"

"Before you what. Come on say it, 'Before you forget'?"

"No, before I have to hurry up and take you to bed."

Jessica takes him by the hand and slowly leads him to the bed. She pulls him down on top of her body and gives him another tongue lashing. Booth is trying to pull his shorts down. She helps him by using her foot to push them to his ankles. Booth hears voices in the living area. The roommates have come back. Booth never had them on his mind. He sits up and pulls his shorts back on.

"Don't mind us; we'll just go to bed. We won't bother you."

Booth doesn't know how long they have been watching. They are already nude as they walk over to the bed in the corner and lay on top the sheet. Booth had only heard of situations like he was in. Jessica can see that he is uneasy about being in this predicament. One man in a room with three nude women. His penis has gotten even harder and is protruding a boner in his boxer shorts. He decides to play it cool and act like he is used to this situation.

"Oh, don't worry, we're through," he tells the women.

"Yes, we can see that you probably made fantastic love," says one of them, smiling and pointing to his hardness.

"Look, Jessie, we'll leave and come back later," the other woman speaks.

"No, that's alright. You stay here. Sandy, I can see that you are inhibited. Let's go up to your room."

"No, we can stay here. This is not the first time I've been in a room with three nude females," says Booth, lying.

"Yeah, I believe that!" remarks Jessica. "Probably as a baby in the maternity ward. Let's go to your place."

Booth had taken up lodging in Yellowstone Park's majestic Old Faithful Inn. In his large bedroom, they make the fantastic love that her roommate spoke about. Lying in bed the next morning. Booth wakes to find Jessica fondling his hair and looking him over. She kisses him in short pecks about the face and neck.

"What's the story on your roommates, Jessica?" he asks.

"Alice and Ginny are homosexual, but aside from that, they are the sweetest, caring, and responsible ladies that I've come across in here."

"That's all well and good, Jessica, but I'd like you to move in here with me. There are forty other couples in the inn. I believe you will be safe here."

"Safe from what, homosexuals? I don't have to worry about Alice and Ginny. And yes, there are other couples in this house, and one is that big black who that hangs out with you and his weasel-looking lover."

"Oh, you mean Lewis. OK, I can see what you mean. Move in, not because I would worry about you being in that situation, but because of me?" he asks. "At least think about it, Jessica."

"I'll give it a lot of thought, Sandy, just as soon as I stop reminding you of your wife."

In the morning Booth leads an exploratory group of 40 from the park up the Mystic Falls trail to the top of a hill where they could see Old Faithful doing its thing in the distance. An hour later they arrived at the Imperial Meadows trailhead and could see the waterworks of Old Faithful even better. They encounter bull elk and moose along the way and have to navigate around them. They pass Little Firehole River near where lava flowed thousands of years before. Along the way they see settlements of inmates whom they had not made contact with. They stop and tell them of the headquarters in the Park. They stop short of actually going into the camp area surrounding Old Faithful. They make it to the top of a mountain and look out at the Upper Geyser Basin where, through hissing steam and drifting mist, they spot the Hephaestian waterworks. Then, as if on a timetable, the grand alarm clock sends a plume towards the sky. They can see hundreds of men just lying on the grounds around the Geyser. There are also hundreds of horses tied up to trees and rope lines. If these men are hostile, they can easily get to the exploratory group. Booth convinces the group to turn back as this might not be the right time to intrude on that camp.

Life in the camp is progressing with harmony. There have been few problems that Lewis or French could not control. They had become like policemen. But the spirit that holds the group together and discourages anyone from creating problems is one of family, of brotherhood, and of mutual purpose. To survive and prosper is the motto that Booth has challenged everyone to work towards. The camp is organized. New members arrive daily. They get introduced to a group leader and are placed in housing and on plots surrounding the park. Planting has been completed in all gardens and fields in the flats. Red has the satellite dish going and TV is available for two hours each night. To conserve the short supply of fuel that was left at the Park, only the evening news is turned on. A generator powers up the old inn.

Booth has met with Webb twice during the two months since their first meeting. The last two entries in the tunnel have not been all that traumatic, except for the change in the layout of the maze. Seems that they are able to move the maze walls around, especially to accommodate moving bodies of dead inmates through the tunnel. Help has come from his meetings in the form of parts to get the water pumping, and the power plants and sewer stations on stream. There have been air drops of medical supplies, more seed, and canned meats and vegetables until the first crops are harvested. Jessica spends most nights with Booth, but still has not moved in. During the day she is with Alice and Ginny working in the gardens near the cabin. Cultivating is a major source of pride and joy for all the park dwellers. from the first days those bean sprouts popped up, to today when corn plants and wheat fields make the park look like the farmlands of the Midwest.

In their garden, the three ladies are using hoes to clean weeds between the rows of carrots. Alice and Ginny are topless to keep cool from the piercing sunlight. Jessica is working in a row next to a hillside.

"This area would be good to plants beans." She continues, "the vines can grow naturally up the hill and we won't need to use poles."

A large rock is in her way. There are holes in the ground around its base.

"Ginny, come help me move this rock," calls Jessica.

She is bending over it, trying to move it, when a snake comes out of one of the holes and bites her on the right hand. She yells as Ginny approaches and chops at the snake, but it slithers back into the hole. Jessica falls to the garden across two rows of carrots. Her body convulses and she foams at the mouth. Alice and Ginny are at her side and become hysterical at what they are witnessing. Ginny screams at Alice, "Go for help. Get Sandy."

Alice takes off running up the hillside towards the inn without giving any thought to the fact that she is topless. Ginny bends over Jessica and holds her hand up to her face and bites and sucks on the wound. The convulsions have stopped, but Jessica is now unconscious. Ginny, noticing that Jessica is not moving, puts an ear to her chest to listen for a heartbeat. It's there as she hears a loud *thump-thump.*

Up on the hillside, Booth and Lewis are talking about a former Marion, Ohio, inmate who plans to lead a group of indigents to the park in an attempt to take over. Marion Prison was the replacement prison for Alcatraz in 1963 that housed the most hardened criminals. Inmates there were kept in individual cells and locked up an average of 23 hours a day. It was after guards were killed in early 1980s during an uprising that Marion authorities locked down all cells and never ceased that practice. Amnesty International, a human rights group, had sued the prison and the state of Ohio to change their practices, but lost in the courts. The result that no inmates were rehabilitated and the threat those could impose on society was scary. Many of the inmates believed that they could turn into mass murderers or chain rapists.

"The word from the grapevine is that they are coming from the middle of the compound and at the rate they are traveling should be here in two days," tells Lewis.

"How many of them? asks Booth.

"Ninety to a hundred."

"Any weapons?"

"No word on that, but they are adding to their number as they get closer to the park," responds Lewis.

Booth is thinking of attacking them before they reach the park, fall back if need be, and then attack in force in the flats below the park. Lewis looks over Booth's shoulder and sees Alice running towards them.

"Things are looking up around here. I hope she doesn't fall from the weight of those boobs," he says, pointing to Alice.

Booth turns to look as Alice screams, "Sandy. Help! It's Jessie!"

Alice stops running when she sees Booth; Lewis and others start to run towards her.

"What happened?" asks Booth.

"Jessie was bitten by a snake. She's having convulsions. Come on, she needs help."

"Somebody get the doc," shouts Booth as they all run down the hillside to the garden.

Approaching Ginny who is kneeling over Jessica, Booth slides to her side and picks up her arm to test for a pulse. It was there but slow and faint. He sees the swollen right hand and begins to suck at the wound and spit out the blood.

"I did that already," Ginny says. "I think she's in a coma."

Doc, as he was called, George Weinstein, is a diminutive former practitioner, convicted for deaths of patients in an illegal abortion clinic.

While he is examining Jessica, Booth pulls Ginny to the side.

"Where did it happen?" he asks Ginny.

"Over by that rock. There are snake holes around it. She was trying to move the rock when it bit her hand."

Booth calls out, "Lewis get some help and dig around that rock. We need to know what kind of snake it is in order for Doc to use the right antidote."

Lewis and three others grab shovels and start digging, after removing the rock. Back to Jessica's side, Doc tells him that all he has is atropine and that he can give her that and hope it works.

"We may need a serum," states Doc, "because I haven't seen this reaction to a snake bite since I was in Africa. But what would an African snake be doing in Wyoming?"

"There used to be a snake zoo up here," Booth responds. "Perhaps they let them go or some got free when they cleared out of the park."

"Here's one," shouts Lewis.

A snake slithers out of a hole towards Lewis. He clamps it down with a hoe.

"Don't kill it," shouts Booth.

Booth takes a hoe from one of the other men and places on the head of the snake, reaches down, and picks it up behind the head and holds it up.

"Anyone ever see one like this?"

"What kind is it?" someone asks.

"That's what I'm asking," Booth replies.

Doc has placed a tourniquet on the arm and paints the wound with iodine, cut it open and is suctioning. Booth walks over and asks Alice, "Is this it?"

"Yes! Keep it away!"

"I've got it," Booth assures her.

"Gaboon viper or maybe puff adder, just like I said," states Doc. "African. Sandy, you've got to get to the tunnel and ask them for an antiserum. I can draw some blood from one of the mules, break it down and try to make an antiserum from the antibodies."

"What's going to happen to her, Doc?"

"Coma for 24 to 48 hours, then she dies."

"Write down that name for me, Doc, and then I'm on my way. Red, try to get a radio message out to the tunnel or the military bases outside the compound that I'm on my way."

Doc scribbles the snake names on a piece of paper and hands it to Red. Booth bends to kiss Jessica on the forehead.

The Capture

The ride on horseback to the tunnel takes 6 hours. Booth is riding with a passion to cut down that time. Red Johnson is able to get on air and call out his mayday.

"This is the radio operator in the compound at Yellowstone Park. Governor Sanford Booth is on his way to the northwest tunnel. He wants to pick up antiserum for an African gaboon viper or puff adder snake bite. It is now 1200 hours and he should be there at 1800 hours. Repeat ..." Red Johnson repeats the message over and over.

The message is picked up within the tunnel by the signal operator. He turns it over to the officer in charge.

"How did they get a radio in there, lieutenant?" asks the signal corpsman.

"They have probably got some geek in there that knows all about electronics. I'll have to call Washington to get an OK. You call the air base hospital and get that antidote."

James Webb is at home, watching the gruesome details of the Saturday Prison Authority report. The phone rings and Webb turns down the volume and picks up the phone.

"Hello."

"Mr. Webb, this is General Worthy."

Worthy is second in command in the Prison Authority system and works for Webb.

"Yes, Bob, what can I do for you?"

"Sir, a message has been sent through channels from the duty officer that Sanford Booth is on his way to the northwest tunnel. He wants us to give him an antiserum that is used for an African snake."

"Bob, it's obvious that if Governor Booth shows up at the tunnel, someone important to him has been snake bitten, African or otherwise. See that he gets it. And, oh, Bob, have the tunnel announcer tell the governor that I would like to meet him next Saturday."

"Yes, sir, I'll authorize the delivery."

As soon as he hangs up the phone, it rings again.

"Hello?"

"Hello, Jim, this is Jinx."

"Jinx, how have you been?"

"Fine."

"What's happening in LA?"

"Plenty. Look, Jim, I have come on to some information that I know you'll be interested in."

"What's that, Jinx? You moving back into my neighborhood to drive down the property value?"

"No good, buddy, I'm hooked on California. But serious, you know that secretary of Sanford Booth, you know the governor that you defended?"

"Yes, Gloria Young."

"Yeah, that's her name. I have been trying to place her face with that name for months. Jim, she's in LA."

"Are you sure?"

"It's her, Jim."

"Jinx, I'll call you from the airport as to when I'll arrive in LA. You pick me up."

Webb calls for his Prison Authority Leer jet to take him to LA.

Booth is down the hillside about fifty miles from the tunnel. He is walking the horse to give it a break after riding so hard. He walks it over to a grassy knoll and ties the reins to a clump of tall weeds. The horse begins to graze. Booth lies down in the deep grass ten feet away from the horse. Six inmates from the group led by inmates from Marion

68

prison are on patrol and stumble on the horse. They run to where the horse is and one shouts, "Hey, there's a horse."

Booth hears them, but keeps his position. He is hidden in the tall grass, but a trail shows where he walked through the tall grass from near the horse.

"Willie's going to like this gift," says one voice.

"Let's take it back to Willie, then he can ride up to the park that we're gonna take over."

The Marion group, Booth thinks to himself. *Lewis must have miscalculated their position. I thought they were two days away.* Booth hears them talking again.

"Say, someone had to tie this horse up."

"Let's look around."

Booth lies still. Two of the men notice the bent grass and walk through towards Booth's position. Booth, not knowing how many are there, decides to find out by revealing himself. He runs hard through the grass and between the two men, knocking them down. He comes out to the clearing, starts to untie the reins, and the other four surround him.

They point knives and a handmade spear at him.

"Don't make another move or you're dead," says one.

"Let's kill him anyway," says another.

The other two run out of the grass, shaking the cobwebs out of their head. Booth speaks up, "I'm Sanford Booth, your representative with the government. I'm on my way to the tunnel to talk with the officials."

"Yeah and I'm President Mokski, the son of a bitch who put us all in here."

"Who did you say you are?" asks another one.

"Sanford Booth."

"The governor who tried to assassinate the president three times?"
Booth did not answer.

"Willie will be interested in talking to you!"

"Let's take him back to camp."

"Look, take the horse, if that's what you want, but let me go. I've got to be at the tunnel in one hour."

They help Booth get on the horse and two of them hold the reins, leading the horse, while the others walk on either side.

"Willie will like this. Now that we got you, all we have to do is walk right into that park and take over."

"Yeah, they will probably just give up when they see we have him," laughs another.

"Willie says they have everything set up and all we have to do is keep them working if they want to stay alive," says another.

"You can have what we've got. We can teach you to do what we've done. Planting crops. Using our old skills to fix things up. Not harming each other and trying to live peaceably," Booth advises.

"Are you doing all that at the park?" asks the lone Mexican in the group.

"That's right. We are making the best of our freedom. Fighting each other is not the answer. We won't starve and we're happy helping one another. In fact the real truth is that I was on my way to pick up an antidote for one of our group that has snake bite. The guards at the tunnel will give it to me. The best thing we have is that I am in contact with the outside and can get the things we need."

"Wow, that sounds too good to be true," responds the Mexican.

"Be quiet, Sanchez," states the thin black man, "Willie wouldn't like to hear that you'd rather be on their side."

"Say man, don't you tell me to shut up, because I bet each of us would like what he's talking about and not have to be hungry all the time and traveling all over the place killing those who don't want to join us. In fact, none of us would be alive if we didn't join up."

"Hey, I'd like that."

"Me too," says another.

They arrive at the camp. Willie, who is white and a convicted mass murderer who slaughtered a California family and spent 13 years in Marion under constant lockup, is in the center of the group of thirty at the camp. Booth visually counts and is relieved that Lewis' information on their number was also wrong. *It wouldn't be difficult to win a fight with this number,* he thinks. Five of them stay with the horse and Booth, while the thin black man walks up to Willie and talks to him. Willie motions for the others to bring him forward.

"What do we have here? The governor. Get him down. Bring him over here."

Willie sits down on the porch of an old abandoned cabin.

"Sit down, Booth."

He does and watches as Willie lights up a marijuana cigarette.

"Those Wyoming cowboys grew the world's best hemp up in the hills. Want a hit?"

"No, thanks," Booth responds.

"You all growing any of this stuff up in that park?"

Booth doesn't answer.

"I want to thank you for making it easier for us to take over your little paradise. I also understand that you've been blowing smoke up my boys' asses about how good it could be if they left me and joined up with you. I won't tolerate anyone screwing with my men. Now tie him to a tree, we'll take off in the morning. And see that my horse, *ha, ha,* gets some food," Willie directs.

Sanchez and one of the other men who captured Booth are taking turn standing guard. Booth sleeps. It is nearly dawn and Sanchez is talking to the other guard.

"No, man, I wouldn't ask Willie that. He'll kill you like he did Albert. Albert asked Willie to let the man go to the tunnel to get that snake medicine. Willie just looked at him like he was crazy or something. Then he choked him to death."

"Ask Willie what?" Booth whispers.

"None of your business, man. Bringing you here got our buddy, Albert, killed."

"If you believe that, then you're no better than Willie," he whispers again. "I think you all want what we have, and I'm willing to offer it to you. Even Willie wants what we have, but he wants to take it. We are all brothers in this compound. The government wants us to kill each other off. The way you are going about it just plays out their plan. We have a new freedom. Those on the outside are surrounded by water. In here we're surrounded by walls. But in or out, we all have freedom. They still pay taxes and we still live off those taxes. All of you can have it."

"You're right man. We do want it that way," sighs Sanchez, "but Willie wants to go in and take over."

"Ever try talking to Willie?" asks Booth.

"That's what Jimmy, here, wants to do. Let's go together, Jimmy, and let him know that there are many others who want to accept the governor's help and do this right."

They both get off the ground and walk over to the cabin where Willie is asleep. As they open the door, Willie is roused and sits up.

"Yes, what the hell do you two want?"

Jimmy starts to talk about all the things that he has learned that Booth will do for them and that he wants Willie to tell everyone that he wants them to do it Booth's way. Willie is incensed as he reaches behind his back, pulls a dagger and throws it into Jimmy's chest. Jimmy falls to the floor. Sanchez bends over him. Willie is now standing over Sanchez.

"Now, get him out of here. I don't want to hear no more talk like that."

Sanchez pulls the dagger from Jimmy and in one swift motion, guts Willie, who bends over to grab his stomach, and as he does, Sanchez pulls it out and stabs him in the heart.

"You're a born loser, man. A born loser. This is for Albert and Jimmy," he says with a satisfied look, as he drags the dagger from his heart to the hole in his stomach.

Sanchez looks outside the door to see if the commotion has stirred up the camp. No one has awakened. But there were some who knew what had happened when they saw Sanchez slip out with the dagger still in his hands. And they feel good about it.

Sanchez walks the horse over to Booth, cuts his bindings, and tells him, "Get on this horse and get out. Willie won't be a problem to you anymore. I hope we can convince everyone to take you up on that help. Anyway, I'll be there during harvest time. You know, my people are good at picking crops."

"Thanks, my friend. I'll be waiting for you."

Booth walks the horse to the road before going into a gallop in order to keep from waking up the camp.

Booth arrives at the tunnel. The horse has broken into a heavy sweat. The announcer asks, "Who are you and for what reason do you approach the tunnel?"

"Sanford Booth," he replies, "did you get the message about the antiserum?"

"Yes, Booth, it is placed outside the door. You are late. The message said you would be here at 1800 hours yesterday."

"It's a long story, but thanks for your help," he states as he picks up the package.

"Mr. Booth, I have a message for you. You are asked to report here for a meeting with Mr. Webb on Saturday at 1000 hours."

He climbs on top the horse and gallops off towards Yellowstone.

The Awakening

At the park, Doc has been feverishly working on making an antiserum of his own. Lewis comes into the inn.

"Doc, Sandy should have been back by now. Maybe something happened to him. Maybe he's dead. Anyhow, whatever you got, you got to try it."

"I think it's ready. I didn't have much to work with, and I don't know if the antibodies are the right ones."

"Doc, you said she had 24 to 48 hours. It's getting close to the 24 hours."

Doc fills a syringe with his potion and injects it into Jessica's arm.

"Doc, nothings happening. She's still the same."

"This is no instant cure, Lewis. Even with the right antiserum, we would have to wait and watch."

It is three p.m. when Booth arrives back at the park. He is walking part of the way up the hill and running until he tires, and then walking again. He had to leave the horse after it collapsed from the hard ride imposed on it. At the main house, Doc meets him at the door.

"I'm sorry, Sandy. She died three hours ago."

Booth hands the package to Doc and moves quickly to the door.

"Where is she?" he asks.

He walks over to Jessica's body and rips off the sheet covering her. The look of beauty is present more than anytime that he had seen her. Doc walks up behind him.

"She never came out of the coma. I tried giving her antibodies, but she never responded. Her pulse just went away."

Doc opens the package and reads the instructions.

"Sandy, this is no good anyway; the instructions say it should be administered before 24 hours. That would be in five minutes."

Booth turns, walks outside, and sits on the porch, putting his head in his lap. Doc fills the syringe and injects the antiserum into the body.

"I always follow instructions," Doc says.

He goes outside to console Booth.

"Doc, please get Lewis for me. There's trouble brewing."

"Sure thing, Sandy, anything else I can do for you?"

"Doc, I never took the time to tell her that she didn't remind me of my wife anymore, but now she does."

"There's something, she forgot to tell you too. She was pregnant."

"Oh-h-h!"

They both hear a sound come from the inn. They turn and run into the room. Jessica's body is moving. Her head is turning. Her eyes open and through blurry vision, she sees Sandy and Doc looking like they just saw someone return from the dead.

"What the hell!"

"Doc, I thought you said she was dead. Jessica!" Booth says as he moves to her side and holds her left hand.

She mumbles words that say, "I love you."

Doc moves to her side and begins to check her vitals.

"It's a miracle. I gave her the shot of antiserum that you brought because I didn't want it to go to waste. It had to be used in five minutes or it was no good. But it worked. I can't believe it. Or maybe my potion worked.

"She's going to make it, Sandy. All her vitals signs are coming back to normal. Maybe it was just a deep sleep."

Doc runs out the door yelling so that everyone would hear.

"She's going to make it. Jessica's alive. Lewis, Sandy needs to talk to you," he says as Lewis goes running by him.

The Finding

Webb arrives at LAX. It is now eight o'clock in the evening. Jinx had received the message to meet him at this time and is waiting for him near the runway. Webb climbs out and gets into the FBI car with Jinx.

"Hello, Bob," he says, shaking his hand. "Tell me, how did you find her?"

"I found her in a nightclub. She's a mud wrestler."

"Was this based on a directive from the department?"

"No, it was just by accident. Anyway, I'll fill you in on the details while I drive."

Jinx's car pulls to the employee parking lot of Al Harley's Club.

"We'll wait here for her. She usually arrives for work around 8:45."

"What time is it now? My watch is three hours off LA time. Oh, 8:40"

"There she is."

Gloria pulls up her car next to Jinx's. Opening the car door lights up the interior of hers and Booth can see her face.

"You're right, Bob. Let's go talk to her."

They both walk over to the driver's side where she is bent over pulling her dressing bag out of the back seat.

"Gloria Young?" Webb asks.

Startled, she tries to get back into her car, but Jinx takes her by the arm.

"James Webb, Miss Young, you know, Sanford Booth's attorney."

She has a look of relief.

"Yes, you are. How did you find me?"

"It wasn't easy, Bob here caught your act and recognized you. Miss Young, we need to talk."

"About what, Mr. Webb? I have a new life. The Secret Service isn't trying to kill me anymore. I've been reading the newspapers and I know about all those agents getting killed. And I know that the governor is in that terrible place and has no chance of getting out, so why do I have to talk?"

Webb tells her, "I'm in charge of the Prison Authority, if you have information that can help get the governor out, I guarantee you that he will get out, no matter what the rules. I haven't given up all this time, and I hope you don't. You're the missing link to this whole mess. Now will you tell us what you know?"

"OK, Mr. Webb, but take me away from this place. Wait," she says as she gets into the car, unlocks the glove compartment, and pulls out a tape cartridge from amongst other music tapes, "we will need this."

They take her to the Century Plaza Hotel. Jinx gets a room and brings his tape player from the car. In the room, Webb listens attentively as the tape is playing and discloses the phone messages, and Webb recognizes the voice of the president's press secretary, Ron Baker, as the one who invites the governor to Camp David. In addition, the tape tells the conversation that Agent Herman had with Gloria as the tape was on because she had been taping her singing. Gloria tells how Herman's men tried to kill her and of the resultant death of her roommate, which she knows was meant to be her. Webb talks Miss Young into going back to Washington with him to testify. Reluctantly, she agrees and asks, "Will this get the governor off?"

"It's all we need, in addition to confronting Ron Baker and getting him to talk," Webb assures.

Back in Washington, Webb has set up military protection for Gloria in his home through General Worthy.

The Escape

In the inn at the park, there is a conference of the group's leaders.

"And Sanchez killed Willie and helped me escape."

Booth is finishing telling them about his capture by the group led by Willie.

"So now what do we do?" asks Red Johnson.

"I'd like to lead a group down there and wipe them out or chase them back into the interior," explains Lewis.

"No, I don't think that's the answer. I believe they are in the same boat that we are. There were too many of them who wanted what we have. I think we ought to send a party out to make contact with Sanchez, if he's still alive, and find out what their intentions are as a group," advises Booth.

"Lewis, get fifty good men, and at daybreak take off for their camp."

"Doc, fill us in on Jessica's recovery. Exactly what happened and why," directs Booth.

"The snake bite causes convulsions. She went into shock and then a coma. Suction was applied to the wound every fifteen minutes for the first two hours. At eighteen hours after the bite, I injected her with my antiserum. Three hours later, I pronounced her dead. There was no pulse, no heartbeat, and she was not breathing. And three hours later I injected her with some of the antiserum that Sandy brought back. Ten minutes later, she was stirring, and a check of her vital signs indicated that she was on the road to recovery."

"Doc, do you still have enough serum for another snake bite?"

"Sure, enough for several bites. But why do you want to know?"

"If my friend James Webb will help me, I plan to get a snake bite, have you inject your antiserum, die, go through the tunnel and have Webb administer the final antiserum, outside the compound. If that works, I can get out of here and clear my name."

"But, Sandy, I can't guarantee that the same thing will happen to you. Jessica is a pregnant woman and there are many cases where pregnant women survive where others have died. And, Sandy, you can't get pregnant."

"I'm willing to take that chance."

Jessica walks into the room, still a little woozy from the illness.

"Sandy," she asks, "want to go for a walk?"

"Sure," he replies. "This meeting is over. Lewis, you plan everything and be prepared to put down any attempts to fight. Make a peaceable connection with Sanchez."

Booth and Jessica walk out of the inn and stroll towards a tree-lined path.

"I have to confess something to you, Sandy. I had planned on telling you about the baby. I hate that you found out the way you did. And no matter what you say or do, I plan to have it."

"I want it too, Jessica. I never had children. You can give me something June wasn't able to. I want to confess something to you. The only time in our relationship that you reminded me of my wife was when I thought you were dead. I was attracted to you, not your looks."

"Thanks, Sandy, on both counts. I love you."

They embrace, kiss, and then hold each other for minutes without moving.

It is Saturday morning and at 1000 hours, and Booth is at the tunnel door. It opens, and the announcer tells him, "Proceed through the maze and through the tunnel. Do not stop walking."

To his astonishment, there are no lasers on and the doors to the tunnel are wide open. As he enters, the door behind him closes, and he continues walking as instructed. Upon reaching the computer room,

Webb is there to greet him. They walk into an office and Webb closes the door. He relays to him all of the developments after finding Gloria Young and of the evidence she had been keeping.

"First, I plan to confront Ron Baker and hope that he talks."

"What if that doesn't work? Even with the tape, it may not be admissible. And all you're going to establish is that I was invited, but still there is the matter of how the frame-up at Camp David was accomplished. Someone has to admit to that," Booth advises.

"Well, in that case, we have got to get Baker to talk. He has to know everything."

"Maybe not. Just suppose Mokski told him that the president asked for him to call, but then asked Herman, in Baker's presence, to cancel the invite. Baker would know nothing. Even when he found out that I kept saying that I was invited, he could have assumed that I didn't get the message in time.

"We need another plan, James. Say, I noticed at one of our meeting that the dead bodies are just passed through the tunnel to the outside. I have a plan and this is what I want you to do—"

Booth fills Webb in on the plan to be bitten and the coma that comes with it. He asks him to be the one who claims his body and to be prepared to give him the injection that will bring him out of the death sleep.

"There is one other thing I need you to do. Check out the case on a Jessica Hill of New York City and into her bosses at Finch and Alexander for insider trading scams. The details are on this note."

Booth tells Webb that he will see him in two days at 1000 hours.

Back at the park the next day, Booth tells Jessica that Webb is going to get him out so he can clear his name. He assures her that Webb is also working on clearing her.

"Very soon, I'll be back to get you."

He kisses her and goes downstairs to where Doc is waiting. Red Johnson is holding the snake.

"Doc, Red, don't tell Jessica what I'm doing. If I don't make it, she'll just think that I lied."

"You sure you want to do this, Sandy?" queries Red.

"I'm sure. Doc, you be sure and administer your serum on time. Red, make sure you have me at the tunnel at 1000 hours tomorrow. Doc, don't send me through unless you can pronounce me dead. OK, Red."

Red causes the snake to bite him on the right hand. The wound isn't as severe as Jessica's, however; it causes the same reactions of foaming at the mouth, convulsions, shock, and then coma. Doc performs the fifteen minute interval suctioning for the first two hours. During the night, Doc, Red, and three others take Booth near the tunnel. Red sent out a message to the tunnel the evening before they left to announce that Sanford Booth was dead and that his body would be at the tunnel for anyone to claim it. At 900 hours, Doc was able to say that he was dead. They took the body up by the door and laid it with two others that were waiting for pick up.

On Sunday evening, Webb is at the White House attending a dinner for cabinet officers and their spouses. A phone message is taken from General Worthy for Webb by Press Secretary Baker. Baker gives the message to Mokski, and he smiles a satisfying grin. Webb is watching, because he set it up to make sure Baker got the message instead of him. Baker walks over to Webb.

"I have some bad news for you, James. We just heard from General Worthy—it seems that your Governor Booth is dead and his body is being shipped to the tunnel. Look, old friend, if there's anything I can do, just call me."

Webb thinks, *He actually did it. He really could be dead.* Webb had intended to show a phony emotion, but his thoughts cause him to really be upset. Mokski walks over to their position.

"Anything wrong, Mr. Webb?"

"Sir, I just gave him some bad news. His friend Sanford Booth was killed in the compound," Baker informs.

"Oh, that's too bad. Probably better now than to live in that unruly environment for years."

"I'd better go claim his body, since he has no family. I want to give him a decent burial," sighs Webb.

"Good night, Mr. President. Good night Ron."

As Webb is walking out, he turns to look back and can see Baker and Mokski clanging their glasses together in a toast.

Doc and the group from the park watch from a distance to see the tunnel doors open and twelve guards step out and point rifles at the four bodies, while what appears to be a doctor is using a stethoscope to determine if they are indeed dead. The guards pick up the bodies, place them on gurneys, and roll them inside the tunnel before the door closes.

"Pray that he is alive," cries Doc, as they turn on their mounts and look back while heading back to the park.

Outside the tunnel exit, Webb is waiting with an ambulance to take Booth's body to the airport. Booth had given him instructions to administer the antiserum at 1 p.m.

"Which one are you here to pick up?" asks a guard, who doesn't recognize Webb.

"That one," Webb states. He points to Booth's body.

"Is he really dead?" asks Webb.

"You relatives always find it hard to believe, don't you?" the guard responds.

The driver loads the gurney and body into the ambulance, feet first. Webb rides up front with the driver as they pull into the airport.

"Where to?" asks the driver.

"That Prison Authority Leer jet on pad 17," Webb replies.

In the air, Webb is in the passenger compartment with Booth's body. It is 12:55 p.m. Webb pulls off the sheet covering it. He touches the neck to feel for a pulse. He feels nothing. Webb injects the antiserum into an arm. He waits for ten minutes, because Booth told him it would take that long before he would come out of it. Webb touches the neck again and feels nothing. He covers up the body with the sheet. He thinks out loud, "I knew this wouldn't work. Now I have to prepare for a real funeral." Thirty minutes pass since the injection. Webb is seated, looking out a window and remembering his friendship with the governor.

"You give up that easy?" He hears the voice of Booth.

He thinks that he is dreaming until he hears it again.

82

"You give up that easy."

He turns to see Booth sitting up on the gurney.

"Governor, I, I thought you were dead."

"I feel like I am."

"You did it, Sandy," he says as he hugs Booth.

"Thank you, James."

"We'll be landing in two minutes, Mr. Webb," the pilot voice comes over the PA. "Buckle up."

"Now you are going to have to play dead until I can be alone with you. Just lie there and don't breathe."

"Got another snake?" Booth quips.

The plane lands and taxis. Webb's chauffeured limo is waiting. Two pilots come into the passenger area and one asks, "Can we help you get the body off, sir?"

"No," replies Webb. "You two go on home, I'll wait here for the hearse, and thanks again for a good flight."

Webb gives Booth a suit of clothes and shoes from his luggage bag.

"Hope they fit. I got them from storage where I've been keeping all your belongings."

They wait about twenty minutes and then get into the limo and drive off to Webb's house.

The Confrontations

In the car Webb tells Booth what he has learned from the Securities and Exchange Commission that Jessica Hill's bosses were convicted of insider trading violations and are in the compound.

"Other employees turned them in when they knew that they had no fear of retaliation from them. They were in the same boat as Miss Hill. It is a matter of court record that Miss Hill was framed by the management at Alexander and Finch."

"Can we get her out?" asks Booth. "Because if it weren't for her, I wouldn't be out. Also she's carrying my child."

"That's the bad news, Governor. If we are able to take Mokski down and have the justices change the law, maybe, just maybe there's a chance for her."

Arriving at Webb's house, Booth sees two men standing in the front. Fearful that they may be agents sent there to arrest him, he asks, "Who are those men?"

"Just members of a protective force. They are guarding Miss Young."

Relieved, he gets out of the car with Webb.

"You two can come in now," Webb orders. "I don't want anyone outside when Baker shows up."

"Baker's going to be here?" Booth asks excitedly.

"Yes, let's go in and I'll give you all the details."

Inside the house, they walk into the library. Gloria Young, Justice Wallingsford, who chaired his trial, Judge Farmer, who replaced him in Federal Court and now has jurisdiction, CIA Chief Bostick, who was appointed by President Morton and who's still loyal to the former president, FBI Head Truman Farrell, also a Morton loyalist, Jinx, and Constable Rhashih who flew in from Tangier to verify to the officials Herman's dying incrimination of Mokski are in the room talking to each other and having a cocktail. Gloria runs to him and puts her arms around his waist.

"Governor, thank God, you're alive," she sobs.

Booth doesn't speak, but pats her head affectionately, as he scans the faces of the group and is reassured by expressions as they all move to shake his hand and greet him. Bostick speaks, "As Miss Young said, we are glad to see you made it back alive. When Webb told us the plan you chose, we didn't know if one or both of you would walk through that door. Gentlemen, Miss Young, let's all take a seat. Governor, Agent Jinx here has helped Gloria fill in everyone here with her evidence, first hand. I invited them to be here after telling them what I could, and as you can see, they were convinced that we have national problem. I have invited Ron Baker here also. He thinks that I want to discuss some leaks that I told him I have information on, or more specifically about the truth of his telecasts on Saturdays. When he arrives, this is what we'll do."

Webb shows Ron Baker into the library. The others are in an adjoining room set up with a speaker that allows them to hear and tape the conversations in the library.

"Have a seat, Ron."

"Did you pick up Booth's body?" he asks.

"Yes, I picked him up."

"What is this information you have about the prison telecasts?"

"I want you to listen to this tape."

Webb plays the tape that discloses the Baker's and Gloria's voices as he tells her of the invite to Camp David.

"Where did you get that tape?"

"I'll answer that later, now listen to this part,"

He plays the part that discloses the conversation that Herman had with Gloria.

"What does this mean? I thought you wanted to talk about the telecast."

"What it means is that you withheld evidence about the fact that Governor Booth was invited to Camp David. And also that Agent Herman was working for the Mokski when he tried to kill Miss Young and when he carried out the framing of the governor at Camp David. Herman confessed to all these facts to me before he died.

"But we didn't know how deeply you were involved until Miss Young was found with the tape in her possession."

"That tape doesn't prove anything," Baker denies. "You think you've got me involved in this thing, but you don't have the right evidence."

Gloria walks into the room.

"Perhaps Miss Young can add to that evidence, or perhaps this man can," Webb says as Booth walks into the room to the shock of Baker.

"What! What's he doing here, I thought he was dead."

"Ready for more?" asks Webb.

The other officials, Jinx, and Rhashih walk into the room and stand in a line across from Baker.

"Meet Constable Rhashih, who was with me when Herman told of Mokski's assassination attempts on President Morton and of the framing the governor. I'm sure you know the rest of these gentlemen. They have heard all the evidence and know of your involvement."

Bostick, Wallingsford, Farrell, and Farmer nod their heads, affirming Webb; at the same time. Baker shows signs of confusion and sits down with his head in his lap.

"Well, Mr. Baker, are you going to cooperate now?" asks Farrell.

Baker looks up at the group and pans from one to the other, and responds, "Yes."

Holding his head in his hands and looking down at the floor, he raises his head and pleads, "But what do I get out of this?"

"Witness protection," replies Farrell. "It'll keep you out of the compound."

"And if I don't agree?" asks Baker.

"Then, because of what we already know, my agents are prepared to take you straight from here to the compound, never to be heard from again. You will simply disappear."

"That's what I thought," Baker grimaces. "OK. It's all true. President Mokski directed the assassination attempts. But he never intended for President Morton to be killed. Just to scare him into resigning, which he did. President Morton wouldn't agree with Mokski on the Deterrent plans. Mokski couldn't wait until he had a chance to be president. Governor Booth's conviction was seen as the catalyst that would cause Morton to give up the White House and everything else, you probably know, like killing the agents who knew too much about Camp David. I have a lot of respect for President Mokski. You all know that what he has done caused this country to turn around financially, the elimination of crime and a better life for all. So what's a few lost lives mean, considering the benefits that we all enjoy." Baker pauses.

"I guess those are Mokski's feeling also?" Booth inquires.

"Exactly," Baker replies.

Webb puts a question to the officials, "Gentlemen, where do we go from here?"

Bostick speaks up, "First let's have two agents take Mr. Baker to his home, get some personal belongings and take him to a witness protection location."

Jinx goes into the foyer and talks to the two agents who had been standing outside of Webb's house. They come into the library and direct Baker out of the house.

"This is the plan we have formulated," Justice Wallingsford states. "First, we have to get the governor pardoned."

"But, Judge, there is no pardon for anyone who has been sent to the compound," advises Webb.

"There is an unpublished provision in the constitutional amendment that directed the deterrent to be built and the new law of the land that provides for pardon for a citizen that is able to appear before the president and five Supreme Court justices. Governor Booth is not in the compound. Given the facts, I see no reason why I can't get the Justices together in two hours and have the governor pardoned. Now I know why President Mokski wanted this provision."

"But Mokski will not pardon me," Booth interrupts.

"Maybe not, but the new president will. I have a plan, and with the help of the FBI and the Prison Authority, justice will be served. Now here is what each of us will do."

In the White House, Mokski is seated and talking to Vice President Reggie Johnson, the first black VP of the United States. Johnson was Speaker of the House when President Morton resigned and was confirmed to replace Mokski as vice president.

"I was just told by Farrell, Bostick, and Justice Wallingsford that this midnight meeting was extremely important. Did they tell you what the subject matter is?" Johnson asks.

"Only that the government was in jeopardy and important decisions had to be made tonight."

"Then why am I here? No one ever includes me in any important decisions," chides Johnson.

"They asked for you to be here, but don't ask me why," Mokski replies.

A White House guard leads the entourage of nine justices, Bostick, Farrell, Webb, and Booth down a hallway towards the oval office.

"You gentlemen and Mrs. Waters and Mrs. Spellman wait for us in this ante room, until we send for you," tells Bostick, motioning to the Justices. "Mr. Webb and Governor Booth, please wait with them. We will go in and confront the president."

Bostick, Farrell and Justice Wallingsford proceed with the guard to the oval office door. The guard opens the door and announces, "Mr. President, I believe you are expecting these gentlemen."

"It's late, so get to the heart of the matter. Why have you called us for this meeting," demands Mokski.

Justice Wallingsford speaks, "Mr. President, the three of us here, a federal judge, the other eight justices, and other cabinets members have received evidence that proves, implicitly, that you were behind the three assassination attempts on the life of then-President Morton."

Mokski has a horrified look on his face.

"That can't be!" he shouts.

"Mr. President, you just said that we should get to the heart of the matter," adds Farrell. "Well sir, you have got yourself into an awful mess. We have no choice but to place you under arrest, pending an indictment coming down in the morning."

Johnson's eyes bulge, as he can't believe what he's hearing.

"You can't arrest me, I'm the president," he says assuredly.

"Mr. President!" Bostick remarks, "We have your press secretary, Ron Baker, and your national security adviser, Bill Carter, in custody at this time. They both have told us of your involvement and are asking for witness protection in order to testify against you. However, Mr. President, before you start figuring out how you can deny to us that you had nothing to do with the assassination attempts or the ordering of the murders of the agents from Camp David or Governor's Booth's secretary, we have a proposal that we wish you would accept tonight," states Justice Wallingsford. "We are requesting your resignation, right now, and I will swear in the vice president."

Johnson is standing now, and looks at Mokski in bewilderment and sort of shakes his head in disgust.

"Now here is the proposal: if the new president agrees, the other justices are waiting outside that door and we will pardon you under the new amendment to the Constitution that I know you are aware of."

Mokski, who was standing, slumps down into his chair. He is thinking about his answer as he looks into the faces of the four men across from his desk.

"You got Carter?"

"Yes, sir," Farrell answers.

"And that weasel Baker. I never should have trusted him. OK, let's get on with it. But I can't stand the thought of this black preacher being president," states Mokski, vehemently.

Mokski signs a statement of resignation. Justice Wallingsford swears in Johnson. Bostick leaves to call the other justices into the oval office. Johnson asks, "Did you really do all they accused you of, Mr. President?"

"I don't have to answer that, and no one will ever know as soon as you pardon me."

Johnson gives Mokski a grin and shakes his head that reflects, "No way."

Mokski stands up and leans over the desk, and asks, "You are going to pardon me, aren't you?"

"No way," says Johnson. "You are going to the compound."

"I thought we had a deal, Judge," Mokski pleads.

"Mr. President. Mr. President!" calls Wallingsford, but Johnson at first did not realize that he was now president.

"Sorry, Justice Wallingsford. Yes?"

"Mr. President, Please. We did make a promise."

"You made the promise, but now I'm president, and I want him to pay for his crimes."

Farrell interjects, "Mr. President, you heard him yourself. Leaving the presidency is the hardest punishment for him."

The other justices walk in with Bostick, who asks, "Are you ready, Mr. President?"

Johnson turns to look at the justices and when his eyes meet with Wallingsford, who nods his head affirmatively, he squares his shoulders and says, "Yes, I'm ready."

The justices all sign a pardon and President Johnson inks his first presidential signature.

Farrell tells Mokski, "Sir, we have agents and a long range helicopter waiting to take you to your Chicago home. We've asked Air Force Two pilots to cut short your wife's visit in California and bring her to Chicago. Your personal belongings and memoirs will be shipped later. These agents will escort you to the helicopter."

Jinx and another agent come forward.

"News of your resignation will break within the hour and will say it was for personal reasons."

Booth and Webb are being led to the oval office by Bostick as Jinx and the agent lead Mokski out. Passing each other in the hallway,

Mokski appears in shock as he recognizes Booth. Booth starts for him.

"You bastard," he cries.

"No, Governor," Webb says as he restrains him.

The president and the justices sign Booth's pardon, and at the same time, they hear the helicopter lifting off.

The Harvest

In the Webb's limo, heading back to his house, Webb and Booth shake hands.

"James, I want to thank you for never giving up. You have been the best friend a man could have." Webb smiles.

They ride for a few miles and Booth is staring into space.

"Is something wrong, Governor?"

"James, I need one more favor."

"Anything, just ask."

"I need you to take me to the airfield and have your pilots take me back to the compound."

"Why?" questions Webb.

"I'm going back. I've got some unfinished business there. We've got a crop to bring in and I want to see my child born."

Webb could see that his friend had a new mission in life. *The compound needs him,* he thinks.

"Governor, I have seen that look in your eyes once before when you would not allow me to quit your case. I wish I could get Jessica out for you, but I can't. This deterrent is working and no one person or any Congress will be allowed to change it. You'll be a free man in the compound. But you won't be able to come out again. Oh, why am I saying all this? You know what you're doing is right. I'll help you even more now. We'll still meet. You just let me know the things you need to make the park work."

"Thanks, James," Booth smiles.

From his cell phone, Webb sends a message to the compound that Booth was on his way back, and asks them to alert the radio operator at the park of his arrival.

Booth and Webb are standing in the steel doorway at the tunnel entrance to the compound. Across the field, about one hundred yards away, is a group of fifty park dwellers. Jessica is in that group. They all cheer Booth's return.

"Well, James, thanks again," Booth says as they hug. "My only regret is that Mokski is getting away with just a pardon."

"He'll suffer, Governor. President Reggie will make sure of that."

Booth runs to the group as they start to move towards him. He meets Jessica and they embrace while being surrounded by a cheering group. Some climb onto horses while Jessica and the Governor get into a large hay wagon with others and wave goodbye to Webb.

The presidential helicopter is landing and causes the dust to blow fiercely. Mokski is shoved out of the chopper by Jinx. He falls to the ground. The helicopter ascends and whips up more dust. As the dust is clearing, Mokski, who is blindfolded, takes it off over his head and sees the helicopter flying over the wall.

"This is not Chicago!" he screams after recognizing the Deterrent wall. "No! No!"

Printed in the United States
30526LVS00006B/503

9 781413 765823